Subtle Censorship

Subtle Censorship

The Use & Misuse of Drug Arguments

Wm. Josepf Cardwell

Writer's Showcase

New York Lincoln Shanghai

Subtle Censorship
The Use & Misuse of Drug Arguments

All Rights Reserved © 2002 by Wm. Josepf Cardwell

Writer's Showcase
an imprint of iUniverse, Inc.

For information address:
iUniverse
2021 Pine Lake Road, Suite 100
Lincoln, NE 68512
www.iuniverse.com

ISBN: 0-595-24841-1

Printed in the United States of America

Contents

The Idea

Subtle Censorship:
the use & misuse of drug arguments

The war-on-drugs assumes all casual users are corrupted equally.

It separates family, love, loyalty, and all positive social structures into protectionist policies, while ignoring the fact that casual users likewise demonstrate all of these qualities. It keeps the testimonial as its logo, and ignores the fact that experience holds no secrets. It calls casual use bad and sobriety good. And ignores that in all practical terms the two are simply different.

Subtle Censorship: the use & misuse of drug arguments presents all known arguments both against and for drug-choice. In the time-honored tradition of *The Federalist Papers*, the book is written from the viewpoint of two virtual opponents, **Pro** & **Con**.

Set within point-counterpoint style two opponents present their best & worse case experiences. The debate between the two fictitious opponents is divided into five areas:

- Censorship by WAR
- HUMAN RIGHTS Censorship
- BUSINESS Censorship
- EDUCATIONAL Censorship
- SOCIOLOGICAL Censorship

The source for this unparalleled collection of arguments includes unique philosophical debate, interviews, magazine articles, symposiums, task force reports, news articles, and a forum of televised debates.

Prologue

Prologue

Or, how this book came to be

Some years back, while watching a daytime talkshow concerning drug-use, it occurred to me that none of the arguments were coherent. There was a heavy bias in opposition to drugs in general, and a stigma for those who used drugs in specific.

Over a series of months, I encountered several other talkshow forums; after-school specials and the like concerning drug-use. The same animated arguments were promoted, but never were any counter-arguments allowed.

Out of curiosity I checked the stacks at several local public libraries. There I found shelf after shelf of books promoting the hatred of drugs, books espousing 12-step treatment programs & other forums for psychological legerdemain, books designed to assist parents in guiding their children away from drugs, books formulated to promote an author's failing career; but no material that coherently approached the subject in an unbiased manner.

I had a vague recollection of a study from 1972 by The Consumer Unions Report on Licit & Illicit Drugs. That report suggested the legalization of non-harmful drugs such as marijuana. Like the 1970's it too had faded into obscurity. And of course, a variety of low-quality tracts, pamphlets and booklets from the underground touting tie-dye T-shirts, paraphernalia & the general counter-culture confusion. Barring a few underground treatises there was nothing in the public forum that gave a fair and balanced treatment of the arguments surrounding the use of casual drugs.

With the introduction by Nancy Reagan, the 'Just Say No' campaign injected a new furor and unwarranted bias into the public arena. Both major and minor news media refused to give balanced treatment to the subject. Not a single journalist could I find who gave fair treatment to the issue of legalization of casual drugs. In fact, there seemed a strong pressure to get on board the bandwagon of pure sobriety. It occurred to me that this approach was either selective ignorance or purposeful censor.

With this in mind, I began to collect arguments, both pro and con, about the use of casual drugs. Over a series of months, I realized that the arguments against the use of casual drugs were stark in their limitations. (For the curious, a summary is presented in the concluding chapter entitled, *Resolution*). Not only were the arguments simplistic, never were they weighted or prioritized. Everything concerning casual drug-use was bad, everything about drug-hatred good.

But this made no sense.

Consider, the war-on-drugs assumes all casual users are corrupted equally. It separates family, love, loyalty, and all positive social structures into protectionist policies, while ignoring the fact that casual users likewise demonstrate all of these qualities. It keeps the testimonial as its logo, and ignores the fact that experience holds no secrets. It calls casual use bad and sobriety good. And ignores that in all practical terms the two are simply different.

And so we come to the present work.

I have structured this book as a debate between two opponents, one pro drug-choice, the other against. I have tried to give fair and balanced treatment to both. Though there is a logical structure to the presentation of ideas, I have labored to make the debate seem as natural as possible.

The ultimate intent of the book may seem to build a case for the legalization of certain drugs, however, my greater intent is this: to present the ideas and voices of those too often dismissed in this debate.

I anticipate there will be a number of readers who are against the legalization of casual drugs. I should warn you, the Proponent's voice may be difficult for you to hear, being as it is at times, sarcastic and condescending. Yet, read attentively and you will note the Opponent no stranger to patronizing claims.

Most people believe there are only two sides to an argument. This is a false assumption, for there is right, wrong, and neutral. This oft overlooked third alternative I have relegated to the footnotes.

I would encourage you to not just read passively, but rather engage the conversation with your own arguments. Perhaps, you will come to see the world in ways you have, till now, overlooked.

Censorship by War

Censorship by War

And so the war begins...

CON: Drugs are the unseen enemy—an enemy from within, an enemy from without. Drug users will destroy our country.[1]

PRO: Your enemy is a phantom, no more than your own personal unsound fear. This drug prohibition should be repealed. Drugs should be sold like alcohol, under strict licensing.

CON: It is not a prohibition, it is a war!

PRO: I will grant you it is a war metaphor whose bad use of language can offer no solutions but violence.

CON: You want solutions, it's simple. All we need to do is capture and kill the leaders. You capture Numero Uno. And you will stop this war.

PRO: My simple friend, surely you must realize, in war, every time you arrest Numero Uno, Number Two steps in. And similarly on down the line. Indeed, Number Two occasionally turns in Number One in order to take their place. This is what you perpetuate by war.

---

[1] **UNSEEN ENEMY**: This statement was made by a Rector of the Episcopal Church become Chair of a local drug taskforce. Note the composite demon evil, the unseen enemy that gives both justification and a sense of purpose to his deeds.

Note also how the mind of others is the implied enemy, while only his own associates are smart and good and bright. Lastly, note how the fight is against the drugs. It makes the game all at once clean and distinct. No people are involved. And the lives of the numerous casual users which his taskforce destroys become dismissive with a nod of the head: "Yes. Yes. My countrymen! The demon evil drug."

CON: Not the leaders then, but the source. We will simply kill the plants where they grow.

PRO: You are cute in your ignorance. And what of the simple reality: Push-Down. Pop-Up.

CON: I do not understand.

PRO: Where you may push-down in Mexico, new growers effectively pop-up in Argentina. Where you may push-down in China, new growers effectively pop-up in the Philippines. Where you may push-down in Canada, new growers effectively pop-up in America.

CON: I reiterate, drugs are the enemy. There can be room for doubt. We are at war!

PRO: You set us to war with people and their families who depend on those cash crops to support themselves, just as every farmer and their family depend on their plant crops.[2]

---

[2] **PLANT CROPS:** Peru and Bolivia both sanction and maintain legal regions of coca cultivation. The Indian Nations who live in these regions have used the leaves of the coca plant for centuries. For example, the Inca tribe uses coca as part of their magical and divine religious rites. Additionally, the Indians of the Andes use coca for its anesthetic properties to quell the hunger, thirst, and fatigue from living and working at extreme altitudes. Coca is sold as a tea in the restaurants.

Over 350 thousand campesinos also rely on coca cultivation to support their families where standard food crops are impractical, unreliable, and non-profitable.

Coca is legally shipped to the United States from Peru and Bolivia. It is refined and sold to medical groups as an anesthetic, typically for use by American doctors in anesthetizing the ear, nose and throat.

However, they do not label these necessary imports as 'war booty'.

CON: But we can stop this war. Simply alter our banking structure and create two forms of cash. One for use in the United States and one for everyone not the U.S. This will stop money laundering upon which the drug trade depends.[3]

---

[3] **STOP MONEY LAUNDERING**: This method of control was formulated and presented by Vincent T. Bugliosi in his book *Drugs in America: the case for victory* [1991 Knightsbridge Publishers NY]

Vincent brags that he was the lawyer who oversaw the prosecution of Charles Manson. Vincent needs to be reminded that any lawyer who couldn't have gotten Charlie convicted probably needs to rethink the profession entirely. After Vincent rails on for many pages about the impossibility of all schemes of stopping drug trafficking [including his own]; declares drugs a scourge; he then closes on a rather lengthy chapter in favor of legalization.

Historically the 'good guys' methods of control have included:

- **Enforcement**: from indifference to intolerance
- **Interdiction**: A.A. equivalents, Twelve step programs, tough-love
- **Eradication**: of the plants, the growers, the users, and their children
- **Military Intervention**: usually to divide up the spoils
- **Incarceration**: see the book, *When the Building of Prisons Becomes Profitable*
- **Interrogation**: that makes the Spanish Inquisition look like a quilting bee
- **Forced Sanitarium Commitment**: see the book, *The Manufacture of Mental Illness*
- **Torture**: tell me it isn't so
- **Murder**: to date the murder of innocent casual users by legitimate police force out-numbers the murder of actual known criminal elements. In short, the 'good-guys' have killed, imprisoned, and maimed more innocent people than the 'bad-guys'. Ops. Sorry 'bout that.

PRO: Don't you think when you get to the point of changing money and banking structure that a little light in your head should come on and tell you that you're being misled? Perhaps we should create drug chastity belts to put over our mouths. And trust our government to keep the key.

CON: More simple than your mockery, all we need is plow in more money, more dogs, more men, more machines, more planes, more cars, more boats, more time, more effort, more jails, more jailers, more guns, more & more & more until we stop them in their tracks.[4]

---

[4] **MORE & MORE & MORE:** Here is an extended list of more.

LIST ONE: if drugs are not eliminated, then

More addiction / more birth defects / more child abuse / more child abandonment / more accidents / more divorce / more dropouts / more emergency-room use / more murders / more rape / more suicides / more teenage pregnancies / more lost worker-productivity / more trash on our highways

LIST TWO: if drugs are not legalized, then

More misdirected efforts / more careless arrests / more mismeasure of mankind / more and bigger budgets to waste / more corruption of judges, lawyers, police, house representatives and senators / more false convictions / more budget-wasting crackdowns / more firing of casual users / more court overloading indictments / more losses of dignity / more murders of casual users / more removal of children from their parents / more restrictive laws / more surveillance of innocent citizens / more prison crowding / more rape / more suicide / more spokes-models looking to enhance a failing career / more usurpation of fundamental rights / and more trash on our highways

LIST THREE: some more morés

More advisory counsels / more blue-ribbon taskforces / more colored posters / more cover stories / more Hollywood movies & T.V. specials / more invasions of countries / more lectures / more polls / more special prosecutors / did those other lists happen to mention, trash on our highways?

PRO: Why don't we just stop it, period? This nonsense I mean. This cosmetic morality of looking like we're possessed of perfect righteous indignation?

CON: We will not lose this War. I am encouraged in my travels by signs that Americans are fighting back.[5]

PRO: Hitler also was encouraged by his people that that The war was going well. But on a more realistic note, my friend, if you can't keep drugs out of prisons or schools, how do you suppose you'll keep them out of the country?[6]

CON: We are toe-to-toe with the Enemy; with the drug lords and neighborhood pushers. It is a battle we must fight no matter how frustrating, thankless, or dangerous.

PRO: We are toe-to-toe with our neighbors. With businessmen and entrepreneurs. It is a business transaction we should allow no matter how bigoted, uneducated, or narrow-sighted you might be. You are wasting the men, money, equipment, and time of the American people. You are sacrificing property, lives, and the children of casual drugusers.

CON: It's still a war worth fighting for.

PRO: It is a sham. It is a disgrace. It is nonsense.

---

[5] **BACK FIGHTING:** This is a paraphrase of a statement made by William Bennett, former Drug Czar. His successor Czar was Bob Martinez. His successor was Lee Brown, former Houston Chief of Police. More recent czars include General Barry McCaffrey accused of a variety of covert criminal acts and John P. Walters sworn in on Dec 07, 2001.

[6] **KEEP THEM OUT OF THE COUNTRY:** For whatever a poll may be worth, many indicate that middleclass Americans are more concerned about fixing the potholes in their neighborhoods than they are about the interdiction of drugs like marijuana.

CON: Your hostility to our national war on drugs is rooted in a general hostility to law enforcement and criminal justice. Legal proponents, like you, take refuge in pseudo-solutions.

PRO: How very Soviet Bloc mentality of you to equate justice with prison terms. I suppose justice as merited rewards somehow fell out of the definition while you were giving free license with great civic courage to rape the lives of casual users.

CON: It is war! We cannot retreat. We cannot regroup. We must not falter.

PRO: Yea, Brethren. Hold to the territory of your ignorance and falter not in your absurdity. It doesn't matter if we win, or even gain anything. At least we're doing something about the problem. See that pile of dust over there? Here's a broom. Sweep it back and forth for the next 120 years. That should keep you occupied. At least you'll be doing something about the problem.

CON: Our drug-war is not just about being busy, or justifying our acts after the fact. It is about our reaction against anarchy, disorder, insecurity, and violence.

PRO: Oddly, this drug-war doesn't seem to be about justice, or truth, and humanity's relevance.

CON: It is about relevance. It is about the *will* of the community. A *will* that demands the banishment of dangerous evils that comes through the drug trade, and drug-use.

PRO: It is an errant *will* of the misguided. A *will* that seeks to hold to a way-of-life that no longer exists, and which has become a mockery of worshipful contemplation, social relationships, and the ideal bonds of democracy. What gets to me is how you remain ignorant of the political process that manages human affairs. After all, peace is not maintained by manufactured atrocities of manufactured wars. Democracy is not secured by destroying liberty. Truth is not gained by condemning people to prison for harmless personal choices like the use of casual drugs.

CON: This war is an extension of our constitution. It is a war to establish a more perfect union.

PRO: The mere creation of war as a resolution to non-violent social conflict is in itself a criminal act.

CON: Our unity is this and this alone: ultimately we will destroy you and your kind.

PRO: You have not united anything, except it be the mockery of our constitution, the mockery of democracy, the mockery of human freedom. You have become an industry of politicized hate. An army of nonsense in reserve.

CON: It is our youth that are our industrial reserve army. The strength of our country resides in our youth. We can not allow them to be compromised by drug-use.

PRO: If our youth are any kind of reserve it is an exploitable one. The strength of our country resides in our nuclear determent force and armed personnel. Not some cliché of child as future. Next week you'll be out screaming about population explosions, while herein, it suits your purpose to speak of youth as a commodity product for Nationalist Interests. Talk about compromise. Which nation compromised its faith in every youth that ever returned from war?

CON: Good men, women, and children are dying in this battle.

PRO: Yes. And we wish you'd quit killing them for harmless personal choices.[7]

CON: It is a necessary and good war. This war will drive home, once and for all time, that we do not misunderstand drugs, but that we understand them all to well. Drugs are the enemy. And that is what this war is about, to make everyone understand that we will not tolerate their dangers.

PRO: If that is true, then our only genuine threat is: American Fascism. For your only understanding is based on creating an enemy to destroy regardless of whether you call it drugs, or inner-city blacks, or the poor.

CON: No. It is you that do not understand. This war is about power. The power of minds. The minds of our youth and our countrymen. Our national policy and legislation are simply there to balance the power.

PRO: This war is not about power, mentally balanced or otherwise. It is an unstable emphasis on ethereal social contexts. What is important is no longer America or Americans, but what a few confused policy

---

[7] **DYING IN THIS BATTLE**: The argument was more along the lines that policemen were dying in the Great War.

Probably the most difficult myth to dispel would be this unsubstantiated belief that there is a thin Blue Line between American Society and Barbarity.

Conversely U.S. Census and other work-related occupational Hazard Statistics show that policing is not even in the top three of most dangerous jobs held. Indeed, the most dangerous occupation in the U.S. is an honor held by Garbage Collectors. Though reasons are not given, I can only suppose that they fall off the back of the trucks or catch their

makers perceive. And their perceptions, without doubt, have been derailed from reality.[8]

---

limbs in the compaction machinery. The next hazardous duty is sustained by firefighters. The most dangerous occupation fighter pilots of the military services are not listed as they are not categorized as civilian occupations.

Consider, the plethora of cop shows which show 20 officers in heavy assault gear bursting through a plywood door only to arrest women, children, and a jerk in his underwear. In respect to 'the mission' only overly protective, it seems outright cowardly.

Alternately, consider the siege of the compound at Waco with David Karresh and his bunch of religious fanatics. When the fanatics started shooting back, the task force fled in terror. As they regrouped over the next days, an order went out for massive equipment to put the odds way beyond their favor. In contra force, consider the LA Riots in which the LA police hid out from the fray. Or in the departmental after-the-fact lingo "withdrew strategically". The so called, *Thin Blue Lie*.

However, comments like "Where's a cop when you need him?" are just as frivolous. For it is historically unfortunate that policemen have not been trained as preventionists but rather as interventionists. Consider, in order for a policeman to arrive on scene a crime must have already been committed before the police can be called. In effect, without walking the beat, whereby they can come to know their neighborhoods, our officers become an impersonal presence, seen as both good and evil by the neighborhoods.

[8] **DERAILED FROM REALITY**, or, **HOW TO PEACEFULLY STRUGGLE:** The drug-war, it seems, has become a struggle in which

- Conflict is primary
- Policy is secondary &
- People are tertiary.

CON: It is drugs that are destroying America, not policies, or policy makers. You are simply trying to detract us from the real issue.

PRO: No distraction is necessary. It is not drugs destroying America, but most simply America destroying herself. A self-perpetuated destruction driven solely by conflict of interests among multiple versions of modernization. It is a battle of vested interests in which facts are neither true, nor false. Because, quite frankly, facts have no meaning. Meaning has come to reside only in current ideologies of behavioral compliance and control.

CON: This is war, pure and plain.

PRO: It is not war; it is an unjust police action.

CON: It's a battle for *hearts and minds*.[9]

PRO: I know at least 97.5 million '*hearts and minds*' that don't want you to win, much less force your antiquated dogma down their throats. Tell me again, your war is a war toward what end?[10]

---

[9] **HEARTS and MINDS**: Do these statements have a strange familiarity to any of you Korean or Vietnam veterans? Perhaps it is another War to end all Wars. Yet, like war against wars, it will end only when the victorious realize their greater evil is not a peace.

[10] **A WAR TOWARD WHAT END**: Yawn. Though it is seldom stated, the rhetoric floats around five platforms of intolerance:

- Mere use
- Teenage use
- Abuse use
- Misbehavior
- Business transactions

CON: We just don't have the right people in charge.

PRO: Maybe. But I believe both Goebbels and Himmler died at their own hands.

CON: Our brave boys-in-blue can't fight drugs with these restrictive laws getting in the way. We need to give them the freedom to act.[11]

PRO: I see what you mean. These great heroic saints of human purity need full discretionary measures. And once the casual user is secured, cuffed, and forced to his knees do you suggest a bullet or nightstick be sent into the back of their skulls?

---

[11] **FREEDOM TO ACT**: This is a paraphrase from one of many. Similar speeches have found their vent in longwinded bravado of shortsighted congressmen speaking to near empty halls, and even simpler emptier heads. A bravado which would have Americans believe that: we are tying the hands of our gallant officers.

Note again how it is the "drug", not human rights, that we are fighting. Compare this rhetoric with a fight against, say marbles or doughnuts. Note how frivolous this becomes. The demon evil marble user. The enemy of the state. In this light even a Yankee doodle doofus should be able to unwind from the timbre of its own badly pitched voice and realize: it is not the drugs they are fighting at all, it is an enforcement of status quo.

Moreover, common sense would have us consider the role of many of the media who go out of their way to feed the flames of hatred like A. M. Rosenthal, William Safire [New York Times], and Sam Donaldson. And as well the talks show hosts Geraldo and Maury Povich.

CON: Quit mocking us. This is war.[12]

PRO: This is insanity. Indeed, if drugs are such a danger to Americans now, how come they weren't such a grave danger in 1900 or 1940?

CON: Because we know more now than we did then. For example, we did not know the effects of things like radiation when we first used it in 1900 or 1940s, and so caused harm that did not show up for decades.

PRO: As far as drugs like coca, marijuana, mushrooms, peyote are concerned we have the same data, the same experiences, the same uses then as now. Indeed, nothing has changed. The casual use of these drugs caused no harm centuries ago, decades ago, and causes no

---

[12] **THIS IS WAR**: Let us examine the war metaphor in a fuller light. Consider War's end. Now consider a Suit for Peace. And now consider the inevitable War Trial that must follow.

In defense of the War Metaphor, it is both necessary and wholly responsible to call for the Prosecution of War Criminals. The prosecutions of hate crimes. The prosecution of drug bigotry.

Current lists already indicate a number of high ranking officers and associates of the State, including: Drug Tsars William Bennett, Bob Martinez, and General Barry McCaffrey; ex-Presidents Ronald Reagan and George Bush.

Oddly, as media pundits, each of them to a fault would deride the irresponsibility of Goebbels, who was in no way different in using words to rouse up his cause than they are to their own unbiased approach to journalism. Indeed, it is not hard to imagine how quickly each of these men will go out of their way to call their own use of the press *freedom of speech*, while trying to keep others from soliciting a different point of view.

And so, to continue with our War Trials, the hundreds of local Henchmen of the Metaphor whose names have been compiled must necessarily be prosecuted and sentenced.

Indeed, did the arrogant warriors of the metaphor think their names and irreprehensible deeds would not be recorded by the innocent? Did they never consider someone might document their crimes against humanity? Did they think that they were above the law? That no witness, date, or crime would stand to judge them?

harm now, and will cause no harm in the future. Abuse and dependence only became problems when the medical community became involved in dispensing their techno-chemicals.[13]

And so the trials begin. Both civil and criminal claims against the terrorists of the Drug War metaphor. And so tumble, the bigots of the State: the irresponsible police, the crimes of judges, the ill-considerate social worker, the bigots of the media, as well as bigots hiding behind the public skirts of mass hysteria.

Ah. But it was a War after all. *Nicht wahr?*

[13] **WE KNOW MORE**: Recalling Sigmund Freud, the father of the science of psychotherapy, who tells us that person's maturity depends upon casting off the fetters of our religious beliefs. Should it be said that because we know more, for example, the mass suicides provoked by David Karresh and his followers at the Waco Compound [or Jim Jones in Jonestown] does the knowledge of unlegislated religious use tell us we must repeal the Freedom of Religion? Indeed, these are but two minor examples of the harm born of religious soberism.

Another example would be WWI, the War between Christian Nations. Tell me then, what is it the sober know more about?

CON: People on drugs cannot think for themselves. They are slaves.

PRO: You mean they are voters, and you'd rather they vote like you.

CON: Not only should they not vote, the right should be evoked by anyone that has used drugs.

PRO: I've heard this before. But let us examine a greater concern, the freedom of religion. You cannot deny that once freedom of religion passed throughout society, people proceeded to engage in all sorts of religious behaviors that Believers of traditional faiths knew to be harmful and upsetting. And yet by the purchase of freedom, the truth of valid religion shows through.

Your drug laws are responsible for the deaths of many people who were prevented from purchasing their marijuana cigarettes as safely as they could tobacco cigarettes. Held at gunpoint a stabbed to death for their money and clothes. This is not drug-crime. This is drug-law related crime that forces users to go to places they normally would not go. Indeed your drug laws allow cops to extort money from drug-users or coerce them to act as informants.

CON: They shouldn't have been buying them in the first place.

PRO: I don't understand why you believe that allowing Drug Enforcement Agents to poison, rob, murder, punish, extort, and criminalize casual drug-users somehow benefits society?

CON: Drug Users asked for it when they used drugs.

PRO: Let me see if I understand. First you say drugs subvert a person's WILL, and therefore the drug-user is entirely unable to control themselves. Now you say, the drug-user is entirely responsible for criminal acts perpetrated against them. Which is it? Are free-will and determinism based on some random astrological conjuncture I haven't been told about?

CON: It is both. A person has both free-will and is determined. The drug-user is responsible for not taking drugs in the first place. Yet if they take drugs, and becomes co-opted after taking them, they deserve whatever they get.

PRO: I take it you find this to be the case for all consensual activity? Thus, you deserve being robbed when you leave your door unlocked. You deserve to be horribly mangled in a car accident because you did not buckle your seat belt.

CON: Those are unconscious accidents, not purposeful behavior.

PRO: I see. Then I suppose the conscious decision to employ police to hunt down casual drug-users, while allowing another hour to pass as kidnappers take off with our children is welcomed news.[14]

CON: You are politicizing the argument. Drugs are not political. Drugs are a dangerous chemical. It is a scientific fact.

PRO: When neither researcher, clinician, or physician can agree on the mechanisms, symptoms, or the experience of drug-use, then what we are dealing with is politics, not science.

CON: People, who cannot control themselves, must be controlled. Drug use takes away control; we are simply acting to avoid political catastrophe and social chaos.

PRO: The denudation of liberty, the erosion of values, and the silting of moral waterways is a consequence of sober subsistence. Integrate

---

[14] CONSCIOUS DECISION: Every hour spent investigating casual drug-user or drug salesman is an hour that could be used to find a missing child. Every trial held to prosecute a drug-user or seller might otherwise be used to clear the court system of its true backlog. These conscious acts of purposeful behavior suppose we will not find ourselves responsible for sanctioning them, simply because we refuse to think thoroughly about the situations we create by our own selective ignorance. How often is it that we as humans allow our ignorance and blind sanctions to excuse us personally, but not those about us.

Oh *Blind Justice*, how you distract my attentions with your dimpled thighs.

drug-taking behavior into normal society and you will see where the natural pursuits of mind can lead.

CON: Not the drug-taking behavior I know about.

PRO: You cannot reconcile your drug rhetoric with everyday experience. Your frozen clichés don't change reality; they simply allow you to live with the fantasy you've chosen.

CON: The State has a monopoly on waging war. It selects its enemies, declares war on them, and thrives on the enterprise.[15]

---

[15] **MONOPOLY ON WAR:** Certain people believe the drug-war to be premised on the idea that scientific evidence exists to support the inherent evil or credible danger of drugs. A rather odd and unscientific posit in and of itself.

Still, let us consider a historical example of similar scientific facts, scientific research, and scientific conclusions.

For example, it is well known that the love of the racial myth so exhilarated the self-esteem and solidarity of the German Reich, that hardly anyone questioned the scientific become the genetic basis for the dangerous Jew.

Such scientific and medical conclusion allowed laymen to embrace the far reaches of the Nazi vision of killing Jews in order "to heal" the Nordic Race.

Of one thing it seems we can be assured. The centuries will press on without any fresh scientific discovery, exacting technological research, or heady psychiatric treatments being able to negate lived experience which demonstrates continuously for centuries of use—marijuana, peyote, and psilocybin—are neither harmful nor addictive.

In fact, the refusal of the psychiatric community to take this observation into account demonstrates precisely that their theories are based on misdirection, fear, and political absurdity.

PRO: Yes, but a state may by its constitution have the monopoly on waging war but that does not sanction the state's self-sating indulgence in violence against entirely harmless personal choices. The government's job, as far as war is concerned, is to protect our national interests, not to protect from us from temptation.

The government is not a benevolent parent, and we are not its children. This war highlights the fact that politicians have no true solutions to the problems of society. That they administer and manage the country based on misdirection, fear, and the leverage of intolerance. What we have to fear are not intoxicated drug-users, but rather self-intoxicated political ideologues.

Indeed, in the international perspective, the ideology of drug control has become a front for counter-insurgency, cold war propaganda, and the covert campaigns carried out in third-world countries.

CON: The U.S. Government must necessarily deal in drugs in order to secure the safety of her people as a nation. Still this does not mean drug-use should be allowed for the individuals of the state. Drugs Lords like fascists, dictators, and other ne'er-do-wells are themselves corrupted. Only corrupt leaders and corrupt nations use drugs to consolidate their power.

PRO: Would you call our U.S. military and police corrupted ne'er-do-wells since they train these drug lords in the means of terrorists' tactics. The D.E.A. who trains them in methods of repressing both student and citizen dissention. The D.E.A. who even themselves oversee the establishment of techniques to suppress labor leaders and politicians who are perceived to be non sympathetic to U.S. concerns?[16]

---

[16] **SYMPATHETIC TO US CONCERNS:** For Example, in the mid 1970s Columbia's various factions did battle with one another [i.e. greedy custom agents and D.A.S. Forces]

CON: No, I would not call our forces corrupt simply because they make false use of a war on drugs. For they are there to advance the mission of democracy. To use police techniques, counter-insurgency, counter-subversion, and political control to bring about positive change. They must necessarily deal in drugs in order to infiltrate the networks whose financial resources, tradecraft, and access to intelligence make them a significant political weapon for the U. S.

---

for control of a major drug shipment. The D.A.S. is the Departamento Administartivo Seguridad, the Columbian equivalent of a militarized F.B.I.

In Peru since 1949 the military has controlled the cocaine industry, and uses the profits for construction of military barracks, etc. Washington supports Peru's violent Civil Guard and violent military because they respond well to U.S. counterinsurgency plans. For example, in 1984 Washington wanted to carry out a cocaine eradication front in the Apurímac Area. Oddly, there is no coca cultivation in this area, but it does correspond remarkably well to the area inhabited by the Sendero Luminoso Guerrillas.

In Argentina, [mid 1970s] that government [via Lopez Rega] announced on T.V. that guerrillas were responsible for drug-use in Argentina. Therefore the anti-drug campaign would automatically become an anti-guerilla campaign. This neat formula was well received in Washington. Thus, the U.S. taxpayer passed over not only money to assist Argentina. U.S. agents to assist in the formation of what we call Death Squads. Thus, under the guise of a war on drugs we helped to train, as well as supply weapons, communications, and other equipment to Argentine Death Squads. All of which were used to assassinate a priest, and thousands of non-drug using citizens as well.

In Columbia, Washington has encouraged officials to extend marital law to the entire country under the rubric of Narcotics Enforcement. That is to fight the narco-Guerillas. Indeed, the U.S. used such a pretense to undermine President Belisario Betancur's attempts to arrange a cease-fire with non-drug associated Guerilla Factions.

In Mexico, Drug War Rhetoric was used as a pretense to crush Peasant Land Occupations and Peasant-Worker Alliances in the southern state of Guerrero. A state which continues under military occupation in order to terrorize the populace in general and anti-government movements in specific. The head of the state police who ran the operation was himself a heroin dealer.

PRO: Why is it these terrible leaders use their drug profits to open public zoos, finance city slum rehabilitation projects, and purchase and support national soccer teams? Where is the evil?

CON: They are only running these legal projects as fronts to launder their ill-gained money from the drug trade.

PRO: Why is it drug dealers can never be operating just out of benevolence for their own people? Even statistical odds tell us this must be the case upon occasion, if not frequently and commonly.[17]

Again in Mexico, in 1978 aided by D.E.A. Officials the Mexican government waged a special War called Operation Condor to poison the lands with herbicides and starve out the Indian Peasants. Even after six months of the operation, American D.E.A. continued to coordinate regular practices. The worst of these practices took place in Sinaloa where American agents proudly oversaw torture sessions, extortion, forced confessions, and incommunicado detention.

For the source of these reports as well as many others see the article *Drugs and United States Foreign Policy* in the collection edited by Ronald Hamowy *Dealing With Drugs: consequences of government control* Pacific Research Institute for Public Policy [pp 137-179]

[17] **FREQUENTLY AND COMMONLY:** The anomaly created by the biased observer is remarkable in its attempt to assign evil as the other person's cause for action, while attributing one's own behavior as ever motivated by benevolence.

Thus, the Mafia must assuredly act only out of murder, terror, and hatred, not out of concern over their people, or of loyalty for their organization. Likewise dictators, delinquent gangs, Nazi Doctors.

Indeed, such an anomaly is generally answered in the psychoanalytic literature as a formation of a Dr Jekyll and Mr. Hyde Complex [a.k.a. doubling, slitting, schizophrenia, multiple personalities, and so on]. As an evil that murders rivals, and as a good that contributes to the culture.

Such errant posits are not necessary of course, when one realizes that evil, like good, is not evoked but based on personal definitions of one's own acts, beliefs, and choices.

CON: That's just propaganda.

PRO: Statistics as propaganda. You may be on to something there. How can you find yourself immune from your own format of propaganda. But I must laud you for your diligence, it is propaganda all right! When U.S. newspapers seek to hide the fact that officers of the D.E.A. systematically lie, cheat, and steal. The D.E.A. operates bogus chemical companies that sell materials and instructions for the manufacture of various drugs. Then they arrest their customers. Yet they don't arrest themselves for mail fraud, coercion, or deceptive trade practices.[18]

CON: Human survival is at stake.

PRO: Excuse me?

CON: Health and Wealth. These are at stake. These are interests that should concern all people.

PRO: So the goal is to eradicate the drug-user so that you can gain by stealing their wealth under the guise of forfeiture?

CON: The goal is to stop the use of drugs, not the drug-user.

---

[18] **PROPAGANDA** [surely you jest]: Janet Cooke, a *Washington Post* Reporter won a Pulitzer prize for her story entitled *8-year Old Heroin Addict Lives for a Fix*. When the story was exposed as a complete fabrication, Benjamin Bradlee, the *Post's* executive editor said—"the fraud is no fraud at all, but due to Ms Cooke's mental Illness."—He tells his interviewer, "We're going to take care of her. We're going to see that she has professional help."

Reported in T. S. Szasz *The Therapeutic State* [Prometheus Books pg297]. Reprinted in *Dealing with Drugs: consequences of government control* 1987 San Francisco: Pacific Research Institute for Public Policy ed, Ronald Hamowy [pg 334c]

PRO: Why? How is it you believe a casual use of drugs interferes with your health, wealth, or political voting habits?

CON: As insiders to Washington, both you and I know why this drug War exists. Let us not be naïve about it. We have seen the statistics about drug-use patterns. People of higher income, occupation, and education have few problems with drugs. But we must still concern ourselves with those of low income, low occupation, and little education who utilize general resources while contributing little to humanity. We do not mind that the lower tiers of society make withdrawals from the shared resources of our country, but when they become leeches on those resources, then this relates directly to the health and general welfare of everyone. This is why immigration is such a controversy.

Drugs may not affect those in the higher socio-economic spectrum to the same degree, but it severely and negatively affects those on the low end of the Bell Curve. Thus, we must wage this War.

PRO: Let me for the moment ignore the implied drug-use pattern. It's an appealing argument, for it implies the higher socio-economic class can buy justice, or engage in pursuits at leisure. Thus, the costs of openly announcing a restriction of drug-choice, in effect, costs the higher groups nothing, they can continue their drug-use patterns. Meanwhile this opens up a number of new methods of policing those at the low end of the spectrum such as search-&-seizure, random drug-testing, forfeiture, pre-trial detention, and the break-up of minority families by placing their children in foster homes.

It also provides a very beautiful role model, that is, to teach minority leaders to lead their own people about on the leash of the drug-hating role model. Yet, even as I laud its intricate political beauty, it seems to me a sinister beauty that does not value individuals or individual initiative. I think in the long-term you will not aid but rather harm welfare.

After all, are not the dynamics of our American industrial life energized by lower socio-economic classes, just as they are guided by the higher? Alas, do these challenges and distractions to overcome, do they extend to leisure-time as well? For instance, should anyone be distracted from their leisure by the challenge of which beer commercial to watch? Or which beer brings forth the most fun? Or which beer a sports hero finds less-filling or tastes-great?

CON: Rituals & Regulations. Every society has them. Every society must abide in order to survive.

PRO: Perhaps. But blanket terms like rituals, regulations, and survival never seem to equate to the whole of their reality but only to restricted aspects you wish to choose to support your beliefs.

The ritual of peyote use by the Native American Church is certainly a well-established ritual, self-regulated and valuable by its history, sociology, and philosophy. Yet this still does not stop the Oklahoman D.E.A. or the Federal Government from harassing them year in and year out, decade after decade.[19]

---

[19] **RITUAL USE OF PEYOTE**: Arizona, Colorado, Minnesota, Nevada, New Mexico, and Oregon, peyote may be used by any bonafide religious organization. In Idaho, Iowa, Kansas, Oklahoma, South Dakota, and Wisconsin, use of peyote is only protected within Native American Church ceremonies. In Kansas, Texas, and Wyoming use is only protected for members of the Native American Church, and Idaho and Texas require some "Native American Heritage" in order to be exempt.

CON: We don't commit to drug-choice because of the logical consequences, which anyone who is reasonable will recognize, are entirely
negative.

PRO: The logical consequence is witnessed in the terrorism carried out by
factions like the D.E.A. These indeed are negative. But the logic
attached to the idea of casual drug-use is no logic at all. Speaking of
logic, I not sure what you think you are buying with your war?
Time? New converts to a better therapeutic religion? Cocoon fantasy for false worlds of sobriety? Or simply hatred in a more subtle
disguise.

And finally, this rather potent demonstration on the current state of
the State of endemic war

See reference to *Federal Native American Church Exemption TITLE 21-Food And Drugs
Administration, Department of Justice PART 1307—MISCELLANEOUS—Table of
Contents, Sec. 1307.31 Native American Church.*

Peyotist beliefs vary from tribe to tribe. They involve worship of the Great Spirit, a
supreme deity who deals with humans through various other spirits. More specifically,
the *Peyote Road* is a way of life calling for brotherly love, family care, self-support through
work, and avoidance of alcohol.

For those interested in more information about the many struggles and advancements of
the *Native American Church*, search on those keywords on the internet.

A young couple about to be sentenced on drug charges [the possession of marijuana and cocaine] horrified a packed courtroom when they swallowed cyanide and fell dying to the floor.

After the probation judge refused to grant probation, William Melton, 27, put a white powder in his mouth and collapsed seconds later. His wife, Tracey Lee, 21, walked over to her husband and patted him softly on the head and then put some cyanide powder in her own mouth…They died in a local hospital. It was crazy. It was as if they were going to the gas chamber, said court clerk Howard Smith. They weren't even going to get a long sentence.

[New York Post November 8, 1980 page 4]

Human Rights Censorship

Human Rights Censorship

Or, by what right will I deny you

CON: Drugs lead people into murder, robbery and other crimes.

PRO: I agree, drugs lead people into crime just as much as Christianity leads people into murder, robbery and other crimes.[20]

CON: What do you mean by that?

PRO: Corrupt drug-enforcement has lead to kidnapping, murder, theft and other crime performed by the very people responsible to protect us.

CON: It has not.

---

[20] **CHRISTIANITY LEADS PEOPLE INTO MURDER:** Here the counter-reference is made concerning fanatical Christian fundamentalist sects like the K.K.K. As well as a plethora of historical incidents like the Crusades, the Spanish Inquisition, and the Holocaust (supported and sanctioned by various members of the Catholic clergy).

Both arguments are of course frivolous. Drugs and Christianity do not lead a person into crime. They are used as an excuse for the crime, just as any State will attempt to justify its own bad acts as 'legal'.

Speaking of states, note that the argument could likewise be extended in light of the history of our own McCarthy terrors, Trail of Tears, Japanese American Incarceration during WWII, political gerrymandering, and business exploitation, to conclude,' Democracy leads to murder, robbery, & other crimes.'

PRO: Yes it has. Not only has the drug-war lead the police into crime, drug money continues to corrupt our law enforcement officials, our judges, and our congress people. [21]

CON: It's our duty to protect the non-user, not the user.

PRO: Harm to self from abuse is unstoppable. Consider suicides and death-pacts. You cannot legislate depression.

CON: We are not trying to legislate depression we are trying to deter crime. It is our right to deter crime.

PRO: True. It is our right to deter crime. In fact, it is a necessity. But when viewed in terms of human rights, deterrence is valid only as long as it does not infringe on our right to engage in socially non-threatening activities. Casual drug choice is no more a danger to society than bunji-jumping, car racing, speed boating, or skydiving.

CON: But drug-use is a danger to society. It is a fact, I read about it everyday, drugs create violence. [22]

---

[21] **CORRUPT OUR LAW-ENFORCEMENT OFFICIALS**: Still, it is my position that such law enforcement officials were corrupt in and of themselves. The money is not to be blamed, but rather the person who accepts the bribe.

[22] **DRUGS CREATE VIOLENCE**: Speaking of violence, consider these proposals that have been made from various sober state legislators concerning casual drug-users:

- Establish artic gulags and banish all users.
- Decapitate all dealers.
- Execution for all salesmen. Automatic. No other act need be involved.
- Suspend Indictments. Take away privilege of council and trial by jury.
- One strike and you're out. Anyone caught doing drugs or selling drugs. Life imprisonment.

After all, they cry, these people are our enemies.

PRO: Not so. In fact, legal drugs eradicate the reason for violence. Violence results simply from the desire to *control the trade*.[23]

CON: The way to *control the trade* is to build more prisons.

PRO: Sixty percent of jail space is filled with casual users. How is this justice? Or even of benefit to us as a nation?

CON: I'm for giving them all the space they need to think about what they've done. Let them rot, if necessary. If that's what it takes to jerk them out of their dead-end lifestyle.

PRO: You've ripped productive individuals out of society for harmless personal choices. And with brave rhetoric this side of the barbed-wire fence tell us that you expect them to learn reformation to your thinking while currently being taught an education by criminals.

---

[23] **CONTROL THE TRADE:** In other words, let's say I offer to buy 3 autos from you. You put forth the upfront money, buy the cars, and deliver them to me. I take the cars and sell them. But I refuse to pay you. What happens next? Well since this is a 'legal' transaction, you sue me in court.

Now let's change the commodity and leave the context the same.

Let's say I offer to buy 3 kilos of hash from you. You put out your money and deliver the goods. I take the stash and sell it. But I refuse to pay you. What happens next? If you take me to court, the judge will say this is an illegal transaction. The judge will tell you, you have no recourse in their court because you are acting outside of the statutes of the law.

Thus, your next recourse is either to beat me up, destroy some of my property, kidnap my family or friends, or attempt some other form of 'justice' which will let me know that you are serious about getting your money.

Whenever anything is made 'illegal' it automatically spawns a whole plethora of crimes, both petty and brutal, that are meant to 'control the trade'. That is, to control a trade that no longer has any recourse to justice in the public courts. In effect, it is private justice set to compensate for the lack of any availability to public justice.

In the case of drug prohibition just as in the case of alcohol prohibition the refusal of the public to be sensible about harmless use has lead to an enormous amount of unnecessary crime both petty and vicious.

CON: We are made safe by our drug laws.

PRO: We are not. People's rights are discarded and usurped where drug laws are concerned.

CON: They are not.

PRO: Then what do you call boot-camps, urine tests, roadblocks, strip searches, and searches without probable cause, preventative detention, and non-judicial forfeiture of property, and on & on...[24]

CON: I call it a good idea.

PRO: Such ideas have forced us to sell our rights for foolish legislation.

CON: There is nothing foolish about a just system.

PRO: But your system is neither *just* nor *right*. Your prohibition is creating the very problems which it chases back round into the criminal justice system.

CON: It does not matter how busy our Justice System remains, that is its job. Our justice officials are not there for rest and recreation.

---

[24] **BOOT CAMPS:** These metaphorically nice sounding boot-camps have historically been called such things as reeducation centers, indoctrination camps, or more simply, prisons.

PRO: When you speak of rest & recreation, you speak to the very problem. You have usurped the rights of adults to spend their leisure time as they see fit.[25]

---

[25] **USURPATION OF RIGHTS**: A division exists between lawyers, judges, and civil officials in the use of 'special laws for special legalities'. This division is important because it highlights the usurpation of human rights. Let us consider the violation of three of our American Constitutional rights, say, for laughs, the 4th, 5th, and 8th amendments.

The **4th amendment** is supposed to guarantee us of right of security in our homes. But busting through doors with fiberglass battering-rams to arrest a casual user seems contrary somehow to being secure in your home. Still, all-in-all don't you love to watch it night after night while ruminating for a snack in between news trivia and sports wa-wa? Indeed, why bother your head with the consideration that houses, boats, cars, are as irrelevant as the casual drug-user's children who are up for auction by the state.

The **8th amendment** is supposed to guarantee us of security from excessive fines and cruel and unusual punishment. And yet, not so unusual are these multi-million dollar fines for a single marijuana plant that hardly equates to a six-pack of beer? OK, a five-pack. Perhaps, it would be less cruel and unusual to fine every owner of a beer can, let's say, at least a million per can. Reasonable right? It is if you're a legal lover of 'special laws for special legalities'.

The **5th amendment** is supposed to guarantee you just compensation for private property usurped by the government. Now consider this scenario. Let's say you happen to rent your home or boat or plane to a nice looking group of folk who decide to grow a pot plant, or smoke some marijuana they brought along. Sorry. You lose.

It doesn't matter if you know what they do. This is forfeiture. A special law that says just because you are ignorant of the special law is no excuse. After all, you haven't done anything 'ill-legal'. Still, there goes your boat, your home, and your plane. Because, after all, the property itself has committed a crime. It has allowed people to put smoke in their lungs.

CON: Government's duty is to restrain evil and promote order.

PRO: I agree it is a government's duty is to restrain evil and promote order. Yet, should the government in the performance of its duties, inflict a greater evil on the target group than the target group performs in society?

Or from a different perspective, should our government justify its own great evil for the moral opinion of a few confused and bigoted citizens?[26]

CON: Drug-related crime cannot be ignored.

PRO: That's right. If a crime has been committed beyond simply using casual drugs, it should be pursued and dealt with appropriately. But I don't hear you railing on about true crime, the crimes of authority figures such as judges, politicians, and police officials. I hear your rhetoric as selective exclusion.

CON: Still, drug-use is a crime.

---

[26] **JUSTIFY OUR OWN EVIL:** The argument is as follows:

- We/the US government are stealing people's property from them in order to fund this 'war'.
- We/the US government are kidnapping children and auctioning them off to the vagaries of the foster care system.
- We/the US government have created millions of political prisoners.
- We/the US government have done all these evils because people have casually smoked marijuana.

PRO: You do realize that your entire argument is nothing more than a misinformed attempt to legislate sobriety. If you cared about crime then you would help to counter **authority-related crime** which exceeds in extent & damage to society all drug-related crime throughout history.[27]

CON: When all is said and done it is still the law. We must obey the law. Drugs are illegal, and that's that.

PRO: It was 'the law' under the Third Reich to burn humans alive in ovens. It was The Law in the 1800s to own slaves. Do you like those laws? According to you as long as it is 'The Law' we should enforce it with blind patriotism, no matter how amoral, how destructive, how vile. It's 'the law'. What a nice sounding phrase, at least for the fundamentally complaisant. Nothing could be more dangerous than therapy, the pesticide of the mind, which has not eradicated but rather spread epidemics of irresponsibility. Still, you are ready to apply its artificial fertilizers against the natural use of drugs.

CON: Psychology doesn't mess with values or the mind, drugs do.

PRO: I would be ready to believe you, but I don't recall such a thing as Eskimo physics.

CON: What's that got to do with anything?

PRO: Well you claim psychology is an exact science. You raise no objections to the hackneyed concepts of a 'Black Psychology' or 'Female Sociology', when by the very characterization of science, science should be 'value free' in its conclusions. But you scream foul play at the notion of 'Eskimo Physics' or 'Female Quantum Theory'. You then blindly turn to psychology and its occult treatment of cure words, its faulted statistical ciphers, and its ritual of programmatic

---

[27] **AUTHORITY-RELATED CRIME**: Crimes of government employees, crimes of judges, crimes of police, crimes of politicians, crimes of priests.

mysticism to declare the 'scientific' existence of deterministic evil in the guise of addiction and addictive personalities.

CON: I believe addiction exists. I believe it has been scientifically proved.

PRO: And I doubt your convictions.

CON: I know its true. You can't convince me otherwise.

PRO: Perhaps. still, I have found the best test between a human aping the opinion of the rank, and a person's own true beliefs is to see how much they are willing to bet on their conviction. I ask you, are you willing to wager a $1? Perhaps $10? What about increasing the stakes to your life? Or the enslavement of your family?

Here's the Test I propose. You put up $100 thousand. I'll put up $100 thousand. Once a neutral party secures that wager, we will flip a coin.

- If it is heads, *you* will choose the casual drug and *I* will choose a person to take the drug.
- If it is tails, *you* will choose the person, and *I* will choose the casual drug.

The drug choices include {coca, marijuana, mushrooms, or peyote}. The person will take a standard dose of the drug, once a week for a year. After the year, they will be asked to stop taking the drug. If they do not use the drug over this second year of our experiment we will conclude they have not been addicted.

Now I ask, are you still ready to wager? But before you answer let me tell you what my choices will be. Given this better Information, surely you will be at a greater advantage in this wager.

If the coin-toss decides you are to choose the drug, I will then choose myself as the tester. If you choose the person, it matters not which of the drugs I choose, for none of these will be found to be addictive. Indeed, the person of your choice is likely to stop taking the weekly dose before the year is over. This likewise would defeat the hypothesis of addiction. Now, are you still ready to wager? Here is an experiment at its most real and most scientific. Moreover, your hypothesis of addiction is no longer a remote TV opera to mimic the politicized opinions of the herd, but a personal arena with your reputation at stake.

CON: The test is unfair. You don't have an addictive personality. You might be able to walk away, no problem, but not so others.

PRO: Just as you are walking away from your 'scientific' contentions I see.

CON: You can't fool me with your fancy dialectic. Addiction is real.

PRO: And I notice that the press and politicians can't fool you with their dialectic concerning drug-use either. Still, the concept of addiction runs counter to the notion of individual initiative. So let me agree with you that addiction is as strong as the initiative of the individual.

From this I am supposing you will observe that either the people of the U.S. are in the majority a bunch of ne'er-do-well, slavish brutes. Or people are in the majority well-behaved, sensible individuals with personal initiative.

The choice is yours, masters of their own destiny, or slaves to therapeutic claims.

I for one do not fear making choices.

Thus, neither do I fear making my own drug choices.

You, to the contrary, may fear choice, democracy, drugs or anything else you are told to.

But let me remind you why I object to the premises of a drug-war, just as I object to all misapplications of political logic. It is a one-size-fits-all conclusion. A one-size-fits-all federal program of social welfare looking to define truth through money economy & policing privileges.

CON: The drug-war may be run by the Feds, but it was borne out of the democratic process.

PRO: How so? When did we go to the polls and vote to make casual drug-use a crime against humanity?

I'm not certain how you can call absolute preclusion, democracy? Since preclusion usurps choice, there is no democratic process. Not only is there no vote, there is no discussion.

There was never any choice give to pursue casual drug-use. It has been legislated into existence by bits and pieces over years & years, by legislators who hardly constitute anything more than a majority of pompous ideologues.

CON: We don't need to vote on drug-use, casual or otherwise. We have pharmaceutical manufacturers and pharmacists, and physicians. Only they are educated enough to handle the sophisticated and complex realities concerning drugs and drug-use.

PRO: Thank you. I never realized here is an entirely novel form of corruption of education.

We must be specialists to acquire knowledge; else our test scores will defeat us. We can not question the soundness of conclusions until schooled in the apropos jargon, and given the special pontifical blessing of a diploma.

You may be on to something here. We should halt the vote because the economics of running a country are too sophisticated and complex for the average person. Indeed, it is too sophisticated and complex for the average politician. We must immediately dissolve the United States government and hand over control to schooled specialists. Thank you for pointing this out.

I find it rather absurd that you think specialists are needed to determine how a person spends their leisure time. Do we likewise need beer experts to dispense appropriate pre-game doses of the alcoholic brew? And marijuana specialists to measure the precise amounts of distilled water for our bongs?[28]

CON: You cannot eat your diploma in the form of cannabinoids and psilocybin.

PRO: I would rather 'eat my diploma' in the form of cannabinoids, than swallow your sober hysteria in order to matriculate into your selective birth of ignorance.

CON: You have no right to use drugs as you see fit; and should be given none.

PRO: I'm none certain what to say to that. I don't understand why you feel drug-use is not a person's personal choice and responsibility. Do you feel your self-esteem will be damaged? Do you feel others shouldn't enjoy themselves least you tell them how? Do you feel you haven't enough emotional Insurance to cover the inadequacies of the personal provisions of your own will?

Maybe you just can't 'help yourself', and you want to extend government intervention as a kind of drug contraceptive become propaganda clinic for those of your same tottering flabbiness? Maybe you feel that the family will be destroyed?

I guess we should go tell the good families of Amsterdam, one of the most pleasant cities on the face of the globe, where casual drug-use has been legal for decades, they can't possibly exist.

CON: Every life is precious; it cannot be wasted on drug-use.

PRO: Life without liberty is not precious. Life without liberty is slavery.

CON: Drugs will make of you a zombie.

---

[28] HAND OVER CONTROL TO SCHOOLED SPECIALISTS: Just to forward the notion of required specialization in complex fields then it should be necessary to turn over child-rearing. For none but the self-appointed seem to know how to make a child turn out correctly.

PRO: Life should not be wasted on sober zombie-ism, but I see no cryptic war against it.

CON: We must protect our children.

PRO: Protectionist policies are fine for children, but we are speaking of adults and adult choice.

CON: If our peace is at stake, then can freedom be far behind?

PRO: Peace and stability are precious. But peace and freedom come from humans who value liberty. Not from those who are hounded into submission, or persecuted for harmless personal choices.

Laws cannot be respected which do not secure the freedom from fear of reprisal, personal safety, protection from arbitrary arrest, and freedom from punishment for non-threatening social choices, including casual drug-use.

The State is neither competent nor functionally sound enough to assume the role of parent. Citizens are not children in need of help or discipline. They are not savages in need of pity. They are not mental defectives in need of coercion. Yet once the State makes its citizens the objects of its 'enlightened' interest, it moves to make them the objects of its pity and its wisdom. But the pitiful wisdom of the State, invested as it is in the legislative and policing authorities, ultimately means coercion. In this regard, democracy is especially illustrative; for democracy exists, not simply because of majority rule, but because it respects minority opinion. When the minority opinion ceases to be recognized, likewise ceases democracy. Majority rule alone is more simply called *hegemony*.

We follow law because it serves our discipline, our repentance, and our guidance. Those who follow law for any other reason are not human at all, but animals who seek to be controlled.

Law cannot make us wise; cannot make us love; cannot make us strong; because law is an imperative of prohibitions, not a process toward ethical development. For this reason alone, slaves to law seek to limit their obligations through legal tactics—especially their moral obligations. Such legal tacticians become responsible only by their conformation to statute & precedent, not by what they should do, or could have done. Thus, legalism's first failure is in self-centeredness. And it's second, is its indifference.

It has always been the case that legalism forsakes the art of humanity. Indeed, never has legalism assisted in the construction of our character through a questing discipline of care for our resources—especially other humans.

For example,

- A farmer destroys his barn to keep fire from spreading to his neighbor's property. His neighbor refuses to compensate the loss.

- A passer-by watches a policeman beat an unconscious man to death. They make no report of the event.

- A man smokes cigarettes all his life. Contracting cancer he sues the cigarette company.

- A woman is raped. Fifty neighbors look on from their apartments. No one calls for help. No one intercedes.

- A worker hastens through their job, shoddy in their work and personae, in order to hurry home and vegetate.

In short—this is social obligation at a minimum, and in some respects much below. Thus, social performance based solely on systematic law undermines both political freedom and personal freedom.

By its culture, *legality* always seeks to hasten its own march toward totalitarian control; it is our moral duty to force legal justice back into line with moral justice. Not by petty attempts to legislate morality; but rather through appropriate sanctions directed against those who administer bad justice

A court is not the last resort or refuge of what is just. It is an institution subject to decay and drift. *Decay*, by its unjust membership; *drift*, by the change in context in time.

My friend always be aware, time makes ancient good—uncouth. And so our uncouth drug-laws.

After all, when the laws of state or religion become more relevant than the law of existence; when the laws of state or religion become more relevant than the law of love & will, then they have failed to give dignity & respect to humanity. And they have given permission for their own fundamental alterations. Indeed do they cry-out for change.

Business Censorship

Business Censorship

Or, what business is it of yours?

PRO: Would you agree mission statements provide valuable information?

CON: Do you wish to tell me Drug Cartels have their own mission statements?

PRO: I imagine they are no less well prepared than any other business organization in their confusion of missions. Nevertheless, the current business metaphor tells us that no organization can even begin to confidently speculate about its mission unless it can answer six simple questions of business:

- Who are their customers?
- What service do they provide?
- Where do they compete?
- What competitors should they respect?
- What is their preference of a public image?
- What future can they procure?

CON: Certainly. Strategic Planning 101. Too easy, my friend. You and I both know:

- A Drug Cartel's customer is the drug-user.
- Its principle service is to create a slavery to drug-use.
- As to competition, every Cartel wishes to compete on a global scale.
- Who are the competitors? The Cartels themselves. Blood-thirsty. Savage. Unrelenting.
- What is the preference of their public image? To remain anonymous.
- And what do the Cartels wish to be like in the future? Most simply, they wish to be more powerful. More wealthy. And in absolute control.

PRO: Curious. I did not know you were a spokes-model for the Cartels. However, I did have something else in mind. Consider then, my friend, for I wish you to speculate intelligently and confidently on a certain mission statement. But before I present that statement, let us review each of these six questions one at a time.

CON: For the sake of argument, why not. Ask away.

PRO: (a) **Who are the Customers of the U.S. War-on-Drugs?**

CON: That is simple. They are the drug-users.

PRO: No. I did not ask who are the customers of the Cartels. I asked, who are the customers of the Drug-War itself. Who benefits most from waging this Drug-War?

CON: I can think of no other than society itself.

PRO: Nice guess, but no. Ask yourself, who profits most from the war on drugs? Who wages an invasion upon profits both human and financial that makes the Cartel attempts seem like a minor sin?

CON: I do not know. Why don't you tell me.

PRO: Well since you dare to know, the major profiteers of the drug-war are:

- The American Association of Medical Practitioners
- Border Troopers & Merchant Marines
- Federal Organizations under divisions of ATF, CIA, DEA, and FBI
- Rehab Organizations
- State & Local Police Organizations
- Tax Revenue Offices
- The major Pharmaceutical Manufacturers
- U.S. Prisons, and ...
- The Psycho-Clergy.[29]

---

[29] **PSYCHO-CLERGY:** In short, the replacement of traditional religious leaders by psychiatrists and psychologists.

Though previous human value systems were based on religious beliefs, over time, our value systems have come to rely more on more on politic, or rather, on the sovereign power of the State, which, like God, holds absolute power over life & death.

In turn, psychology has become the *de facto* Religion of State.

In any event, it is theology that still holds sway over our acts, beliefs, and choices. Indeed, theology enables our ethic, view of life, and education.

Now it does not matter whether that theology subscribes to a **cult of god** [theism proper], a **cult of man** [atheism, law, politic, sociology, science, technology], a **cult of mind** [philosophy, psychology], or a **cult of nature** [mother earth religions].

CON: In what sense do you make such a claim?

PRO: They very definition of a customer is based upon the concepts of sense, service, and satisfaction. In the current scheme, the only persons who are recognized served, and satisfied are not persons at all, but precisely these organizations. Let us call them the **Profiteers.**

As customers of the U.S. Drug-War, the Profiteers are sensed of central importance. Daily are they served the confiscated resources of casual drug-users.

They are satisfied by seeking new & improved legislated seizure techniques on Local, State, and Federal levels.

As customers, they need never prove their own need for a product. As long as the Profiteers can take home the treasures they most desire—seized property, seized boats, seized planes, seized bank accounts, and seized humans, whether as children placed into the foster care system, or, adults placed in to treatment programs. The Profiteers are happy to be rewarded by the selling of these things.

Accordingly the Profiteers' insatiable need for satisfaction to seize property and freedom, allow them to dive upon humanity as their

---

The pattern of behavior will be guided by a chosen theology.

Unfortunately, the sanctioned theology of the State, *psychology*, is based on some very unsound and limited concepts. Least such a claim sound too broad to be delimited, here is a short list of some of the more limiting aspects of the theology of the new therapeutic membership

- the psycho-clergy subscribe to the infantile notion of all-or-nothing addictions
- they subscribe to an ideology [more at *false ethic*] based on conquest, not education
- they have no concern for ultimate matters
- they have no training in self-criticism
- they apply emotional relativism to the point of irrelevance
- they adapt their methods to political platforms, not human values

savory victim. Thus drug-use must be propagandized as evil, as bad, as undesirable; else, the Profiteers would not be able to obtain self-quieted absolution for the wrongs they perpetrate against humanity, much less, the causal cruelty they perpetrate against the casual drug-user.

How can the casual drug-user be of consequence? None in humanitarian terms, plenty in the wrongful highjacking of the casual drug-user's property.

"We are not the inhumane ones," the Profiteers claim, "We are saving children from drug-use."

All the more curious, don't you think? For children should not be allowed to use drugs than to drive automobiles. A puerile argument which slaves the notion of children to drug-use in order to disguise the fact that casual use of drugs by adults has never had any ill effects on society.

Indeed, the customers of the Drug-War are the Profiteers: the A.M.A., D.E.A., the Feds, the I.R.S., the U.S. Prisons, Pharmaceutical Manufacturers, and the Psycho-Clergy.

CON: You go too far with this metaphor. It is the drug-user that needs to be bankrupted. They are the evil. They use drugs. They deserve to have their property forfeited.

PRO: And what of prescription drug-users? Should they not also be ready to forfeit their property for their sins of drug-use? Why only government-sanctioned drugs?

Let me supply you an answer.

Most simply, government sanctioned drugs are paid for by political clout through pharmaceutical manufacturers and their political action committees, who are more commonly known as PACs.

It seems then the only good drug is a drug that is sanctioned by our government in order to regulate our health and dietary laws.[30]

CON: The reason pharmaceuticals are sanctioned, as you say, is because the pharmaceutical companies spend years in research and testing

---

[30] **HEALTH AND DIETARY LAWS**: Abused drugs can cause some nasty problem, for the abuser and those close to them prejudice and ignorance being the most notable.

As to the physical problems they may be as complex as the symptoms associated with say a bad toothache—insomnia, nausea, vomiting and diarrhea, mild increase in blood pressure, loss of appetite, dehydration, & loss of bodyweight.

Of greater moment than any of the naturally occurring drugs, are the **problems associated with physician prescribed drugs**

- allergic reactions
- depression, repression, & mania
- tissue, organ, & liver injury
- poisoning
- as well as a variety of side effects like sleep disorders.

Not to forego such problems as

- physician misdiagnosis
- physician mis-prescriptions, and
- and the inevitable lawsuits for malpractice

For an overview of pharmaceutical drugs and their attendant physical complications, that is prescription drug problems, rather than natural and physically safe drugs such as marijuana, mushrooms, peyote see Sydney Wolf *Best Pills, Worst Pills* Public Citizen Health Research Group, a nonprofit organization founded by Ralph Nader in 1971. Public Citizen Box 19404 Washington DC 20036.

Best Pills Worst Pills lists 120 standard drugs as well as over 600 actions, including double and triple interactions. Additionally, the current year's *Physician Desk Reference* offers a synopsis of prescription drugs, their interactions, and complications though you may need to consult a medical dictionary against some of the terminology.

Unfortunately the large-scale problems created by prescription and chemically manufactured drugs have been wrongly associated with natural substances such as marijuana.

under rigorous conditions. Moreover, there are strict regulations overseen by various government agencies that regulate the manufacture of prescription drugs.

If we legalize all drugs then we will have to accept all new freebase drugs introduced by Asian and Central American Cartels.

PRO: Though I also disagree with the manufacture of non-naturally occurring drugs, let us examine your argument. After all, new products coming on the market must stand or fall on their own. They exist under the same economics of supply & demand, as any other product. Moreover, you have neglected to consider the process of quality control which every food & drug item must necessarily follow on its slow introduction to market.

I am always surprised how you fanatics think economics is some kind of free-for-all. Do you not realize that even the Black Market is self-regulated.

CON: Perhaps. But it is you who does not realize the cartels will offer more & more progressively exotic and dangerous combinations of drugs and they'll do it 24 hours per day, 7 days per week. To any age, and on credit.

PRO: So you think they'll purposely kill off their own clientele? Even, if you were correct in your absurd claim, all you have argued for is legalization, regulation, and quality control.

CON: Now you're just being silly. Legalize everything and we will legalize things that we cannot treat. We are not miracle workers, there are services, including treatment and cures that cannot be provided. Not only are we not prepared for treatments, the cost of clinics and personnel would bankrupt our country. I don't want to foot the bill to supply treatment programs and free drugs for people too poor to afford them.

PRO: Though I would be happy to support honest treatment programs, I too do not wish to pass out drugs, just because someone can't afford them. Neither would I distribute automobiles, clothes-dryers, or staplers just because someone couldn't afford them.

CON: You cannot convince me, I will not foot their bill.

PRO: I don't want to foot the bill for this drug bigotry you're disguising as enforcement.

CON: Even were I to agree with the legalization process, and I will not; still, drugs will retard the progress of our society.

PRO: Thought processes such as yours when placed into committees may retard the progress of our society; and yet society itself and business health is not determined by any one small aspect of decline, even that dumped on the casual use of drugs.

In truth, the state-of-health of our way-of-life depends on wide, divergent, and independent institutions. Only if the majority of our institutions were sick could society fall to stagnation or decay.

Indeed, drugs enhance the progress of such institutions as medicine, biochemistry, education, pharmacy, pharmaceuticals, research, sociology, and a list of hundreds more.

Your argument is spurious in the least, and foolish in the larger part. If drug-use could collapse America or even her morals, indeed, if something so trivial could lead to her decline then, quite frankly, she wasn't worth much to begin with.

CON: Perhaps. But even if we legalize drugs, the cartels will undersell the government.

PRO: You expect the government to sell drugs? Perhaps, there is a degree of insanity in your training. Casual drugs, when legalized, must undoubtedly be placed in the open market, under the care of private businesses.

CON: Granted that the government should not sell drugs, but even if the U.S. granted licenses to sell drugs, the profits made by the cartels would be obscene if we legalize drugs.

PRO: Doubtful, but even granting your argument, so what? Is not free enterprise about profits?[31]

CON: Legalization will profit the drug cartels as they are already in business.

PRO: Legalization will drop profits—everyone will be forced to vie for a restricted market. Legalization will drop their profits because the price of drugs is inflated by 10-fold increase. Moreover, the buyer will no longer be deprived of 90% of the purchasing power of their money without any net economic benefit through taxes accruing to the economy as a whole.

CON: People who deal in drugs are ruthless. They will not give up their shares in the market just because drugs are legalized.

PRO: There's always a supply of amoral people looking to make a quick buck. They do not need drugs to be ruthless. You must separate the few who as people are themselves corrupt, from the greater number of people who are not.

CON: I tell you again, if we legalize drugs, drug-use will spiral out-of-control.

---

[31] **PROFITS:** Is this a political or business fear, or both? If so, the argument would run—because the drug cartels already have large investments, production, transport underway we could never catch up to them. The counterargument then runs—American businessmen are lazy and fear competition. The argument is also made—the government gets jealous when left out of grown-up business ventures.

Historically, America has kept tight reigns on her southern continental counterparts whether it be drugs, oil, or bananas. For one of the numerous accounts see Walter LaFeber *Inevitable Revolutions: the United States in Central America* W.W. Norton & Co Publishers 1983.

PRO: Consider for a moment, a single cargo plane carrying 100 metric tons of cocaine would supply the entire American continent for one whole year.

One plane.

Now, I do not tell you this to point out the folly of trying to catch the tens of thousands of planes that fly in each year. I tell you this because there is a plateau of use. In this case 100 tons supplies all we need for a year.

In free enterprise, you can't force people to use more, if they don't wish to use more. That plateau must be shared by all manufacturers who wish to make a profit.

The only reason the cartels can continue now is that our unjust laws make the prices unreal. Once legal, the price will drop. Only a few groups will be able to meet costs of manufacture, transport, and marketing. Just as there are but a few beer brewers who must vie for the plateau of alcohol sales.[32]

CON: But the cartels also operate legalized prescription drugs. They flood the market with Valium, Percodan, and all the other uppers & downers. Legalization has not eliminated those markets.

PRO: Perhaps, but considering money is legal tender for all transactions, why do people still sell counterfeit bills? After all, a variety of humanitarian organizations hands-out bibles for free, and yet, this does not stop the distribution and profit from counterfeit bibles for profit.

CON: We're talking supply & demand here. Supply of social ills. Demand for rehab & education.

---

[32] **FREE ENTERPRISE:** There also exists the argument that a drug dealer's earnings reflect the extraordinary risks of the trade, just as the wages—for example, of stuntmen and high-rise construction workers—reflect the risks of their trades.

PRO: We're talking supply & demand all right: supply by free choice and demand for quality control.

But I have allowed you to lead our discussion astray. Our current focus is not on the cartels, whose profit is miniscule; but rather on the Profiteers whose profits are multi-fold. Again we must remember those who benefit greatest by the drug-war are the Profiteers: the A.M.A., D.E.A., the Feds, the I.R.S., the U.S. Prisons, Pharmaceutical Manufacturers, and the Psycho-Clergy.

Knowing this, let us examine our second strategic question.

(b) What are the Drug-War's principle services? Would you care to venture a guess?

CON: I need not guess. The principle services are:

- Freedom from the slavery of drug-use
- A violence-free society
- The elimination of criminal activity, &
- The recovery of our impressionable youth

PRO: Again you need to reconsider. The U.S. Drug-War's principle services are to the Profiteers. The principle services provided for the Profiteers are:

- Political Manipulation
- Child Slavery
- Forfeiture Profiteering
- Prison Labor
- Support of the first state-sanctioned religion—psychology.

CON: Relativism is not the only thing that abandons truth, philosophers like you love the slow crime their mouths bring into the world—a gospel of misdirection.[33]

PRO: It is true that the gospel of the philosopher is by no means dead. It was not buried with the past, nor did it decline with the great empires. It rises in each new generation wearing the familiar guise of remembrance. I remind you again, that inhumanity has not passed from this earth.

CON: Why would you say our drug-war's principle services are to the Profiteers? How you can possibly misled the facts that drugs like alcohol & nicotine already cost us in abuse-related accidents, and health complications. They cost us in increased insurance costs and lost time on the job.

The fact you should learn is that drugs are a disservice to our businesses. Drugs decrease the skills of our workers, and therefore the productivity of our nation.

PRO: Not true. The drug-user who has long training in both states of mind is actually a more efficient worker. The development of a person's skills depends on the state of mind at the time of their training.

Consider, my friend, a person can be trained as well to perform any task on drugs, as not. Just because a person has spent twenty years trained in sobriety to perform their tasks, from contemplation to construction, should tell you that studies which test people only superficially trained an hour, a day, or even a month or two, while

---

[33] GOSPEL: [from L. god good + spell tale] (1) Something accepted as an unquestionable truth or guiding principle, (2) A doctrine that is believed to be of great importance.

under the surrogacy of drugs, are themselves faulted and unbalanced. Not self-conclusive.

Such productivity studies are in defect, not drugs, nor the drug-user.[34]

CON: That is patently absurd. Science would be absurd to make such claims. Indeed, science would no longer be science, a neutral

---

[34] **PRODUCTIVITY LOST:** Because no study can validate worker productivity declines in direct relation to drugs, the productivity rhetoric is adapted to statements like—in compliance with applicable law.

The primary objective is to meet federal, state, and local com-pliance regulations, so that insurance rates will be substantially lessoned, outlets can be provided when lawsuits are filed against on-site accidents, and in a few cases bided jobs can be obtained. One such government compliance regulation is outlined by the Department of Transportation's Title 49 CFR, part 40 and Part 199.11

Other government agencies besides D.O.T. who sweep in their own sets of regulations] include Occupational Safety & Health Administration, and state variants on a theme like Cal O.S.H.A., California's local occupational hazard.

Note that companies such as petroleum refiners can search & seize at will any person, or object {e.g. car, lunchbox, briefcase, shoes, etc} while on their property without warrant, without warning, without even commonsense.

Random testing pools are also enforced for contractors, & subcontractors entering these facilities. Thus, drug testing itself is a major cause of productivity declines. As it costs in excess of $1000/person/year and requires up to 8-72 hours per person downtime (without pay) for the worker being tested.

In the case of such companies as oil refineries, which each use 1000s of contractors & subs each year, this sends lost productivity costs above the billion dollar mark. Note how it is unrelated to casual use of drugs, but rather the testing itself that propagates its own problems, costs, and downtime.

Such testing groups like D.I.S.A., Drug Intervention Services of America, along with similar groups rake in millions from such unnecessary tests, while simultaneously holding up laborers, act as the primary contributor to thousands of lost man-hours, and millions of dollars in lost wages each year. Year in and year out.

observer, but a consensual expectation formulated on the empirical bias of political activism.

PRO: Science does not mirror reality. It mirrors repetitious observables. What does not fit the clockwork is not allowed. Thus, the compiled information from the social sciences deals with statistical regularities. Therefore, the sciences do not mirror society, but only the repetitious observables of a society. And anything which is not repetitious automatically stands out like a sore thumb.

Now consider. Because society has driven casual drug-use into hiding no repetition can be observed. This leaves only the odd character like the inner city teenager to promote the social image of the drug-user.

There was a time when frenzies and mass emotions could be drained away, and dispersed through religious devotion and practice. Now there is only secular humanism and therapeutic religions. Both of whom need a demon evil against to weep and wail. Since these new formats of worship can posit no heaven, and no god outside themselves this leaves only the pursuit of minds different from their own.

The impulse to exhaust restless energies against unknown and unrealized evils is still strong. It now has its aggressive outlets directed against drug-users. But even if all drug-use were to cease, even then, the energy would still remain to create another abstract evil against which to rage.

Those who see drugs as evil mimic the behavior of a young angry intellectual; they can not define the content of the cause they seek, but the yearning is strong and clear.

When religious belief dies for a person, that person predicts the death of spirit for all people. When illumination died for the sober fanatics, likewise, they came to predict the death of the mind for all.

What are the sole profits of the drug-war, if not the material gains of the democratic criminals who oversee its pursuit, who now have a name. They are the Profiteers.

Now I ask that we examine the third of our questions about missions,

(c) Where do the U.S. Drug-War Profiteers contend to compete?

CON: This is elementary; we will compete on local levels. On State levels. On National levels. On Hemispheric levels. On Internal levels. If drug-users ever make it into space we will compete on Universal levels unknown to humankind to keep them from the use of drugs.

PRO: I am certain you will try. I applaud your dedications. But I am not comfortably reassured you are reasonable in your quest. But in truth you compete against resources of human potential.

CON: The only potential for those who use drugs is prison, reform, or death.

PRO: Human minds are not limited resources to be thrown in jails as though they are simply another thought to be marked as subversive and added to Catholic Rome's *Index of Forbidden Books* or Japan's *Institute for the Investigation of Barbarian Writings*. People must not be subjugated to mind censorship and formalized condemnation because primitive minds of primitive politic tell them they can or cannot learn this or that way. [35]

My intention and my focus is this, not to just explain simply why the drug-war is wrong, but to explain correctly why it is wrong.

CON: Do you contend you will legalize drugs simply because you tally your own propaganda a major instrument of war?

---

[35] **BARBARIAN:** In the tradition of things purely Japanese anything non-Japanese.

PRO: This I cannot answer: It is like asking of a successful politician whether his heart, lungs, legs or head contributed more to his success. When all along the success was none other than the convictions. And so naturally you lead me to my fourth question

(d) Who are the competitors of the Drug-War?

CON: Will you tell me Interpol?

PRO: Apparently you already have the capacity to tell yourself anything you wish to believe. But I would find myself in a life-long battle to try to create trust in a traitor.

CON: The only competitors of which I know are the drug-users themselves, as they compete for the next jail cell.

PRO: Very colorful. However the competitors are the Profiteers themselves. And to date, it is fortunate that they do not compete among themselves, otherwise you would see even a greater greed and greater horrors of your endemic war on drug-users.

But allow me a question, how can you trust a person whose code of ethics it is not to trust you?

A reasonable answer would be, you cannot trust such a person. Consider then, how can you trust these institutions, the Profiteers, whose code of ethic it has become to not trust you?

CON: I will say this about you; you are colorful in your art of words. But I have no problem trusting the Profiteers, as you call them. They have served us well. They will continue to do so.

PRO: Since the initial purpose of this endemic war is steeped in mystery and sustained without purpose, held without acknowledgement of costs, and renewed without realization of any expected benefits, let us not argue the soundness or lack thereof of such a notion, but rather let us note that even if there had been some political intent behind this war that is no longer the case.

CON: You fear we are winning our war.

PRO: I fear what you fail to promise—a future that is more than the presentation of destruction for destruction's sake. Allow me to add to my observations the following rather obvious aspects to your warfare.

- There are no decisive battles to be had
- We are at war with ourselves to affirm values that no longer exist
- It is a war in which the war booty funds no economic or social diversification; but rather only rearms the military operators
- We are at war with 1/5 of the nation
- Like our nuclear determent rationale is a war premised on all-or-nothing strategic doctrine

Indeed, nuclear war and our drug-war share on common theme that is abhorrent only to those who still possess their humanity, a doctrine of total destruction of a way of life different from their own.

CON: I would agree the life of a drug-user is different from my own, as different as night and day. For one, I am a productive member of society, the drug-user, on the other hand, has never been nor never will be a productive member of society.

PRO: Go tell your president and other powerful users of casual drugs how much more productive you are than they. And while you are at it, also remind them in this glorious posturing for a war, America suspends her very reason for existence,

- Her beliefs in the sanctity of life; as long as it is not the drug-user's
- Her respect for the rights of the individual; but not for 1/5 of the nation the casual drug-users
- Her tolerance of minority opinion; as long as it is not the casual drug-user's

- Her acceptance of choice; but not the drug-user's, or their family or their friends

- Her accountability for her acts; but not against the ransacking of homes, theft of property & possessions, & the enslavement of the children of the drug-user

In other words, America's war-on-drug-users has come to the point that she has subordinated democracy to coercive therapeutic legislation based on a conqueror's all-or-nothing ethic of assured destruction for the personal choice of casual drug-use. Quite a conundrum, indeed. Yet ever so rewarding for the Profiteers.

But sense you cannot see this, steeped as you are in the image of a drug-war as beautiful in its destructions, let me ask you the fifth of my six questions,

(e) What preference do the Drug-War Profiteers prefer to find as their public image?

CON: Let us at least agree the U.S. Anti-Drug Coalition is a benevolent humanitarian, a global philanthropist. We can be no other than correct in our concern, and assured in our goals.

We have at our disposal not only the image of a society of democracy, but the spirit of a greater good.

PRO: I agree that a future based on a world-wide totalitarian oligarchy is no better than your benefice, but still I am confused.

Consider again with me, if you will, the modern witnesses and executioners of scholarship of which you speak—your pundated media, formularies of politicians, masons of priests, & sets of psychologists—have come ready to select and organize patterns it is true; but these selections are based on patterns of opinions, and provide no relation to a history of actions. They are convenient to their present purpose. And that purpose has been simply to serve as a normative model for behavior.

In short, they are convenient stereotypes.

CON: What's wrong with that? Aren't you at least democratic enough to allow those who know best to do the best job at controlling the world?

PRO: No.

CON: Why not?

PRO: Because they act only according to purpose; not according to reality.

CON: I do not understand.

PRO: And that is precisely the problem.

CON: Do not play your word games with me.

PRO: In short. What are the objectives of the Profiteers?—*destruction of anything of which they do not approve.* What are their strengths?—*propaganda.* What are their weaknesses?—*truth and good deeds.* What are their reaction patterns?—*fear, violence, and indifference.*

CON: The National Socialists had an awful habit of putting many of their own unattractive emotions into words. But even more so, they developed the more ruinous habit of then printing the words.

PRO: I prefer to think that as long as casual drug-users keep to the strategic initiative of the truth of their own personal experiences, they will remain in the position of power. What concerns me more, is how immensely difficult it must be for you to follow the politics of an underground evil you yourself occupy.

CON: Our interest is to take-away drugs from drug-users. In fact, what if I told you I believe in drugs. But only those we can accept on politically based acceptance, guided by medical science, approved by federal regulation, and sanctioned by the voting public.

PRO: Then I would ask of you our last strategic question

(f) What does the drug-war Profiteer wish to be in the future?

CON: As far as you may hope, out-of-business. No longer managing their product's life-cycle.

PRO: I should think your wish would be to reduce your own terrors, so they will not become better at being the mirror image of you, an alert brute.

Consider, is it not a foolish thing to ask Americans as your drug-war asks them to be strong in bitterness, constant in hatred, and casual in cruelty.

Such is the rhetoric of your endemic war. A war that already shapes your National characteristics and moves its champions toward a more subtle hatred.

CON: If you believe all we sanction is hatred that is your concern alone. Our long-range goal is a concomitant to what we deem necessary to support them. We are committed to the degree that you can bury your own drug-using dead, whether it be under the spiritual, psychological, logical, or scientific inconsistencies by which you live.

PRO: When men draw up an indictment against an entire value of human experience, it becomes obvious that what they wish to banish is not an evil, for evil is self-created and personal. Indeed, what they wish to banish are thoughts that exceed the power of their own. Which part of life is not suffering correctly for your disclaimer?

CON: I don't care. I hate drug-users. I will vote to spend any money necessary to get rid of them.

PRO: Interesting, passionate, but my friend, irrational. Listen, each dollar we spend on drug reinforcement yields seven dollars in economic loss.

CON: How can you say that?

PRO: The drug-peace dividend alone could fund job assistance for child-care & economic development of the poor class which we now group together with the stereotype of ne'er-do-well.

CON: They are ne'er-do-wells. The government always knows best.

PRO: Excuse you?!

CON: Governments don't need to be audited or monitored. They make the best decisions for the greater good, and should always be respected. Especially in times of temptation.

PRO: Tempt yourself with this: choose any state or federal department at random, go audit its budget. Make sure you are sober enough to understand what waste you have encountered.

CON: I am undeterred. Sober is right. We will destroy every drug-user, casual or not, as necessary in order to claim the order we seek.

PRO: When we began, I asked that you answer to simple questions and so you have done. Now I present a mission statement.

The mission statement that I earlier asked you to speculate upon both intelligently and confidently begins like this,

We the people of the United States in order to create a more perfect union ...

My question is this, has the excessive consumption of human resources, human potential, & human dignity by the drug-war profiteers created a more perfect union?

My answer is direct and true—*no it has not.*

Educational Censorship

Educational Censorship

Or, why should I learn your bad habits?

CON: We need more education for our children.

PRO: Teaching children slogans, and how to turn their parents in to the police is not education, it is propaganda.[36]

CON: Those slogans are not propaganda. They represent the mood of frustration and fear that is plaguing our country, growing every week.

---

[36] EDUCATIONAL DRUG POLICY vs. EDUCATIONAL DRUG PROPAGANDA: Of course drugs should no more be sold to those under legal age, than should alcohol or cigarettes. Indeed, schools should consider an adoption of a standard policy concerning drugs such as the following (adopted from a guideline suggested by the Department of Education in Australia):

- Each school should formulate a drug policy in consultation with staff, parents and students.

- Each instance of drug possession or use should be considered individually and independently according to the given set of circumstances at the time.

- The individual using drugs should not be excluded from the supportive resources that exist in the school, provided that the welfare of the remainder of the school population and the community is not jeopardized.

- Teachers and all other employees of the school system should convey by their actions and teachings that they do not in any way condone or encourage harmful drug-use.

- Schools are responsible for preventing, within the scope of their power, the illegal activities of persons who view schools as a means of access to a large number of young, inquisitive, impressionable, and vulnerable people.

PRO: Yes and you are the arrogant creators of that foul mood.

CON: We cry out because once legalized, there will be a potential loss of our inner-city youth.[37]

PRO: You are wrong. There would not be a potential loss of youth, but rather a gain of their trust and faith. Once drugs are legalized, our youth could not profit by drugs. Moreover, youth could no longer

---

- Premature action on the basis of rumor should be avoided. The names of students who are suspected of harmful drug-use should be kept confidential until suspicions are confirmed, and investigations should be conducted as discreetly as possible.

- The best procedure to identify an unknown substance suspected of being a drug is to check with the local pharmacist, police or health inspector.

- Following confirmation of drug possession or harmful use, and following professional consultation, the individual concerned should be provided with an opportunity to select an appropriate form of counseling and treatment.

- While there are many individuals and organizations in the community offering a variety of services related to drug matters, schools are encouraged to establish their own local resource networks.

- Principals, student counselors and teachers should be fully aware of their legal and professional responsibilities, and with the issues that concern the confidentiality of teacher-student communications.

- Drug education should be part of a planned, continuing and comprehensive health/social education program.

- Any decision to suspend a student should be made in accordance with the Education Regulations and in keeping with a stated school drug policy.

[37] **WHY ONLY INNER-CITY YOUTH?** Ever wonder why the drug rhetoric assumes close ties with inner-city youth. Consider. The war-on-drugs ideology borrows heavily from the notion of the Fall & Decline of the Roman Empire. In this scenario it is assumed that the city is glorious. The city can never die.

The city, by default, Must live forever! Else, all true civilization will surely fade away. Charmingly naïve, of course, and yet, a perfect starting point for an ideological war.

tout drugs as a creator of their irresponsible acts. Instead the true source of irresponsibility would be apparent. [38]

Unfortunately, this war ideology separates the history of a city's slow decline from casual demonstrations. It ignores a city's misuse of resource structures, unflagging obsolescence, regional competitive ability, unemployment, net out-migration, and misused funding (to name but a few sources of decline). Instead, drug-use, and drug-use alone is the problem.

And woe be to the social scientist who will not accept this 'judicious' posit. In turn, the drug-war ideology assumes the most easily corruptible city citizens are the youth. Thus, the concept of inner-city youth.

Since the Glorious City knows nothing of lack of opportunity or poverty, the decay of the city must necessarily be related to use of drugs. It cannot be a lack of food that leads the inner-city youth to inattention, anxieties, and lethargic initiatives. For the Glorious City is ready to provide for anyone who is willing to work for it.

Never could the lack of respect be associated with youthful restlessness, youthful revolutions, or inner-territorial wars, it comes only from the selling of drugs. Drugs the ideological evil which leads the youth of the inner city astray, while at the same time, keep the middleclass habituated to female paranoia & male indifference.

[38] **TRUE SOURCE OF IRRESPONSIBILITY:** Which apparently would be what? To keep it a simple list (for there seems no end to those who truly know the source for irresponsibility), literature can be found suggesting any one, or all, of the following:

- Foreign Cultures (more at *Immigration*)
- Hollywood
- Lack of Individual Initiative
- Mediocre Parenting
- Middleclass Insouciance
- Religions (that is to say, just the wrong one's, of course)
- Rock & Roll
- Sex
- Therapeutic Doping
- Television Programming
- Washington DC

Of course, the one point for blame is never the person themselves.

CON: But government cannot nod yes to drugs and urge its citizens to just say no. It undercuts our efforts at anti-drug education and would be fatal to our victory over drugs.[39]

---

[39] **VICTORY:** Peace, victory, reason and happy conclusions for all concerned.

Note the beaconwords.

Beaconwords are to human nations what high-watt flood-lamps are to moth nations. Whereas the moth nation dances around the 100-watt incandescent lamppost of their lives; men's beacon of activity wings round an equally starry wattage of vague & ambiguous ideas.

Ideas that are all-at-once, insubstantial & satisfactory, fuzzy & reassuring. An incandescent beacon to bump our heads against as we dance our philosophical savagery round & round the bonfires of our nights in an attempt to yodel & dance the moon down.

In layman speak; a beaconword is simply a word or phrase that preserves the fuzziness in our dilemmas. A word that reassures our middleclass minds that a capable victory can only result in peace, happiness, and reason.

Which by the way are three prime examples of beaconwords.

Peace, happiness, and reason. All-at-once insubstantial and satisfactory, fuzzy and reassuring.

Beaconwords link humans back to themselves. Give them both positive and negative connotations to hang on a word banner. A pronounceable flag which waves proudly before its lone solider reassuring them that somewhere beyond the rainbow are millions upon millions of like-minded citizens ready to die by their side as they fight alone any unseen enemy that would dare question whatever the beaconword might mean to them.

Sometimes beaconwords are not a single word at all, but a phrase of sorts. For example, *The American Dream*. Ah, *The American Dream*.

Not at all like the Dream of the Unicorn [which is two levels beyond reality].

But a solid & substantial thing—*The American Dream*.

The very same dream that each and every last American—if they are an American—from Pilgrim One to the most current birthed child would agree upon, right? Right.

My American Dream goes something like this—I think your American Dream is wrong.

And there it is.

PRO: You are right. Government must take a stand on one side of the issue. Either *just say yo* or *just say no*. And at the moment the government should quit using drugs in other countries to barter for political goals, while telling its citizens they can not make use of them.[40]

As to your Issue of 'education', I think you have tripped yourself up. Your adjective 'anti-drug', tells us directly that this is no 'education' at all. This is propaganda, pure and plain.[41]

The whole thing starts to stumble when even one long solider of us steps out in front of the banner. Bright lights shining on the vulnerable Ideals in our head.

And if the mass agrees—we're heroes; but if the mass disagrees—then we're ultimate demon evil that needs to be taught a thing or two. (And I've seen the 2X4 that can do it.)

And lastly, allow me to note, beaconwords are quite distinct from the minor incantations called catchphrases. Whereas a catchphrase is similar to a beaconword in that it acts as an envelope into which many concepts are stuffed, altered, and occasionally replaced. However, **catchphrases** are not rallying points around ideas that have specified aims.

[40] **U.S. BARTERS FOR POLITICAL GOALS**—Hooked on drug dealing: As but one example, the U.S. government guarantees India and Turkey that 80% of our opium purchases will be from these two countries. The additional 20% is supplied by Australia, France, Hungry, Poland, and former Yugoslavia. The authorized purchases are made through—Johnson & Johnson, Penick Corp, and Mallinckrodt, Inc.

[41] **PROPAGANDA:** I would have to agree with this observation. Again, these arguments are alignments to causes, not an attempt to educate ourselves about drugs. The term anti-drug says it all, just as anti-black, anti-freedom, anti-dignity, tell their own tale. So consider then these terms: drug choice, drug-use, drug prejudice, drug hatred, drug bigotry, drug phobia.

A great deal lies in the terms and not the condition. Indeed, without an unrestrained dynamic, that is, without unrestricted examination and use, there is no education. For 'education' that cannot be applied, for 'education' that does not leave one with a choice-in-action is no education at all. It is but clumsy propaganda.

To not understand this, is not to understand freedom, but simply accept what is given.

CON: Let me educate you. We are talking about people who murder new-born babies, eviscerate them, fill their bodies with heroin and have them carried across international borders in the arms of women who pretend to be nursing them.[42]

PRO: Are we now? I thought we were talking about people in kevlar vests and riot helmets who tear down our neighbor's doors with battering rams, terrorize mothers & their children by shoving high caliber weapons in their face & screaming blood froth into their ears, plunder houses, kidnap children, steal all hard-earned property, and, one-by-one auction children to state 'care-facilities'.[43]

But perhaps, you do not care to hear about the D.E.A. who auction all possessions to the public and then buy larger caliber weapons, more kevlar vests, and more battering rams to break down more doors and terrorize more citizens and steal their property, kidnap our children, and haul them off as political prisoners of the state.

After all, go enjoy your academic argument and ignore this reality. The depth of ignorance costs you no more than the labor of three generations you have bastardized. Sleep soundly. Keep to the right side of the street. And don't take no gruff from the ruff. After all, someone somewhere is smoking a doobie.

CON: I will not dignify that with a comment. Drugs steal away human potential. Drugs destroy families and friends.

---

[42] **NURSING IDEOLOGUES**: This is a secondhand testimonial from a now dismissed scholar of ethics at Boston University. I withhold the name, as I cannot confirm the event as tutorial or restatement of irrelevant curriculums.

[43] **CHILD SLAVERY AS STATE POLICY**: If it were not the D.E.A. who performed the act it would be called Child Slavery. Cut to militia in full-battle array, child in one arm, an automatic weapon in the other. Overdub: a mother's sobbing. Queue up to child slave in the arms of the D.E.A. agent, trying to quiet her mother's fears, "But mommy, aren't they trained to be terrorists?"

PRO: Nor do you dignify humanity by your purposeful declinations of responsibility to your criminal actions. What destroys families and friends, what steals away human potential is drug persecution.

CON: You now fatigue my attention.

PRO: By your very manner you tell the world that drug persecution fatigues the spirit of common sense. Indeed, you drug bigotry is sustained so you can fulfill the common mediocrity of your sober complacency.

CON: So you would wake me from my sobriety? I tell you now, most sober, most directed, drugs squander our precious resources both spiritual and economic.

PRO: You neglect to consider what you squander by your inhumane actions. Consider my friend, if you've never tried casual drugs you have no right to be arguing. For you would know that what you are saying is absurd. And if you have tried and abused them, then you have no right to try to pawn off your irresponsible behavior as a failure of society.[44]

CON: I don't have to steal to know it's wrong.

PRO: Even if you knew what was wrong, this does not mean you know what is right.

CON: Even if I grant you your argument, children are the victims of drug abuse.

PRO: Are these gang children? Middle class children? Malnourished Paraguayan children. Seems a rather blanket statement. Try this

---

[44] IRRESPONSIBLE BEHAVIOR: Indeed, this does seem to be a problem. When youth try a drug like marijuana they discover for themselves that all this education is in fact propaganda. There is no loss of control, no great demon evil, and only mild stimulation of the mind. Herein is the dilemma—it is hard to respect an authority such as parents, teachers, institutions, and governments who constantly lie to you.

one. Children are the victims of hurricanes. How about: children are the victims of bad political legislation. How about children are hurt when you haul away their parents who happen to enjoy relaxing and smoking marijuana. Indeed, they are hurt. They are hurt by the State. It is the State auctioning children on the block. All in the name of your drug bigotry.

CON: You should have to count the 36 bullet holes in the shattered corpse of a 3 yr old who happened to get in the way of his mother's drug crazed boyfriend.[45]

PRO: You should have to spend an equal amount of time in jail with the tens of thousands of political prisoners you sent up for 30 years for growing a pot plant in their back yard. You should have to work hard labor at twenty cents per day to repay for their houses you stole, their automobiles you stole, their clothing you stole. And you should be beat every day in penitence for kidnapping their children and auctioning them off to the vagaries of state sanctioned institutional foster care.

---

[45] DRUG-CRAZED TESTIMONIALS: Consider & compare:

- Children mauled by pit bulls
- Children killed by traffic
- Children falling into swimming pools and drowning
- Children drinking poisonous cleaning products

Any of which, shown by national statistics year-in and year-out openly demonstrate to anyone who would bother to look them up, publish them, read them, examine their notions, in-and-of-themselves have claimed and maimed more children's lives, year-in and year-out, than anything remotely related to casual drug-use throughout all recorded history.

CON: If we legalize drugs we are sanctioning irresponsible behavior.[46]

PRO: Do you ever sleep at night, or does this abstract fear just keep the nightmare going throughout the day for you?

CON: If not our children, at least we must think of our teenagers.

PRO: What you must realize is that both adult and teenage traffickers already think of themselves as good. They see themselves to be acquiring the ideals touted by political groups such as Hollywood and Washington.

CON: So, are we simply to allow our youth to become corrupt by drugs?

PRO: No more that you would allow them to become corrupt by your bad advice.

CON: Quit mocking me.

PRO: I do not mock you. I simply refuse to grant you the authority to raise idiots and criminals based on your inadequate preparations within reality. I suggest you re-examine the boundaries of your own responsibility.
I further suggest you stop your subsistence to mediocre leadership.

CON: We need leadership, mediocre or otherwise, least our youth become a mass of our own unconsidered projections.

PRO: The young already have their leaders. They no more rebel against a Nation of Teenagers, than a Nation of Mediocrity would rebel

---

[46] **IRRESPONSIBLE BEHAVIOR:** This, I believe, is one of the core feelings of the adamant prohibitionists. They feel that their way of life will be destroyed. That some demon evil mass will go on rampage and destroy the 'very fabric' of social morality.

Though this is difficult to imagine in any reasonable frame of mind, you can certainly see how it would seem quite 'sane' in a frame of sober mental hysteria.

In truth, the release of life from alcohol prohibition demonstrated a gradual return of humanitarian acts.

against itself. The young do not equate illegal with immoral. They equate illegal with hard to get adult fun.

CON: You are sanctioning illegality.

PRO: No, I am not. Consider, America has laws for the protection of human life and America has laws for the execution of human life? Does this sanction murder?[47]

CON: You suffer the soul to advocate the use of drugs.

PRO: Those who suffer are the casual users. And they suffer from the immoral brutality of your amoral D.E.A. hoodlums and plebian fanatics.

CON: Our drug-war is not propaganda, and the D.E.A. are not criminals

PRO: There you are wrong, my friend. You lack a clear and deeper perception of the problem. It is a war metaphor that lacks anything relevant to do with education about drug choice.

CON: Drugs serve for nothing educational

PRO: Actually, the drug experience serves as a means to bring insight into the life process.

CON: No one needs that kind of insight.

PRO: That insight is called intellectual freedom.

CON: Drugs are not an educational tool. They are a menace.

---

[47] **EXECUTION**: 'Crime' is legally broken down into two formats:

- *maleum in se*: in itself bad
- *maleum prohibitum*: prohibited

The bad in-and-of-themselves crimes include burglary, murder, rape, robbery, theft. The prohibited crimes are things like public welfare crimes, civil offenses, regulatory offenses, gambling, traffic offenses, smoking in the boy's room, jaywalking, drug possession, and so on.

PRO: Drug education is only a menace to those who attempt to learn the truth. You and your colleges are safe enough in your propaganda. What you fear is what experience proves.

CON: I fear nothing.

PRO: You fear drug choice. You are conditioned to be sober. Your training is incomplete. So fear you do.

CON: I do not need to depend on drugs for my education.

PRO: Actually you do. In our culture, all people are dependent on education, whether through sobriety or surrogacy. For education is all-at-once a social status, a social contract, and a means toward human equity. To deny drug choice, is to deny these freedoms at their most fundamental level.

CON: I do not need the abstraction of drugs to make my mark on the world.

PRO: You more than most need training in the use of casual drugs. For you have no basis for the imitation of others within yourself.

CON: I am an individual, independent and strong. And that is enough for me.

PRO: You are an individual in action against other individuals within a definite social order. Thus you would be wise to note: You as an individual are nothing. Society as itself is nothing. Only when you alternate them, is the good, the bad, & the bland of each made clear.

CON: Well as an individual, I know drug-use is wrong.

PRO: You know no such thing. You only know that you are instructed to believe in a certain manner. What you encompass is not learning, but education as practical hypocrisy.

CON: It may be practical hypocrisy, as you say, but social control is necessary for ordered morality in the community.

PRO: Absolutely. Social regulation is necessary for ordered morality in a community. And casual drug-use helps to amend that tradition.

CON: Drugs do nothing of the sort

PRO: What then do you call your resistance-to-change, your social mimicry and your drug-bigotry, if not social manipulation become social control?

CON: I call it a defense of sensible values.

PRO: The false notion that only your values lead to truth, beauty, and good, is far from an ennobling thought. Value comes through our quests, not through your pro-active drug-bigotry and state-sanctioned drug-hatred.[48]

---

[48] **VALUE:** value resides in three common quests—truth, good, & beauty. American culture pursues these quests through the following vectors:

- In Science & Technology, the primary quest is for what is true. The Latin term for this is **verum.**

- In Ethics & Religion, the primary quest is for what is good. The Latin term for this is **bonum.**

- In Aesthetics & Spirituality, the primary quest is for what is beautiful. The Latin term for this is **pulchrum.**

Thus, one can establish a variety of value systems based on good. For example, Utilitarian Shangri-la's. Value systems based on truth; for example, Logical Positivism. Or value systems based on beauty; such as demonstrated by the philosophy of Naturalism & Hedonism. You can even create value systems based on a combination of two or more of these.

For example, if we take the values of good and true, we can create a system of Happiness, as have the new therapeutic & sentimental love religions. Alas, that is for another treatise.

But in no case is truth, goodness, or beauty a property of our acts. In reality, they are only assertions granted through useful relations and context. They are not a commodity. They are not a property of our actions. In short, they are not attributes but rather a quest.

CON: I am smart enough to determine my own values.

PRO: Perhaps. But apparently you are not wise enough to know those values depend on whoever determines the philosophy of the state. And that is not you.

CON: I may not be wise in all things, but I know there is nothing about drugs that are educational, whether that education is social, technical, political or simply my own self-awareness.

PRO: Is that so? Let us consider just a few cases in each of these educational arenas.

SOCIAL EDUCATION never talks about

- Use of beaconwords as activation symbols. For example: country, flag, logo, hero, drug-war.
- Use of the *Legacy of Armageddon*. For example: hell is drug-use, heaven is *Disneyland*.
- Use of *Ideological Agents* as a substitute for Faith. For example, the false assumption: what we are doing is scientific.

TECHNICAL EDUCATION never talks about

- Dangers of Pharmaceutical Manufactured drugs
- Purposeful misclassification of casual drugs as dangerous

SELF-AWARENESS EDUCATION never talks about

- Potential increase in cognitive abilities
- Potential increase in self-control
- Individual responsibility intimately bound to both surrogacy or sober states

POLITICAL EDUCATION never talks about

- Censorship & Political Imprisonment of casual drug-users
- State-Sanctioned Child Slavery & Property Forfeiture
- Authority-related crime[49]

CON: I take no comfort in these types of education.

PRO: That cannot be helped. For like a child you have reached an age where you believe you are powerful because (a) you learn only what you choose to learn and (b) the secrets you keep in your head allow you to separate outer action from inner responsibility.

CON: I am responsible.

---

[49] **AUTHORITY-RELATED CRIME:** there will always be crime, and the need to deal effectively with crime. However, the most barbaric, brutal, and violent of all crimes is that crime which indifferent citizens call 'some corruption' and newspapers tend to ignore altogether. More realistically called: authority-related crime.

Authority-related crime is crime perpetrated by judges, lawyers, police, & politicians.

Authority-related crime exceeds in extent & damage to society all other categories of crime combined.

Authority-related crime is the most savage of all criminal activities because such persons are the representation of ideals of society. So by despoiling those ideals, they despoil not only value, but also authority and authority's expectations & consequences.

Bribery, blackmail, coercion, conspiracy, cover-ups, embezzlement, espionage, fraud, framing, gerrymandering, greenmail, privateering, political retaliations, rape, racketeering, reprisals, redlining, sabotage, sedition, sex harassment, tax evasion, & extortion. Note how closely related it is to positions of authority.

Note how little attention is given this aspect of our society, as newspapers give pretentious vent to distractions of 'drug-related' crime while purposely ignoring this more realistic, more common, and more damaging criminality.

Authority-related criminals are least likely to be punished for their bad acts. In many cases, they are further rewarded.

PRO: Then why have you never questioned the skills, expertise, and knowledge required to educate yourself about drugs? For it is extremely difficult to educate yourself about drug-choice, while excessively easy to remain a spectator of state-sanctioned ideological propaganda. How many of these arguments have you ever encountered except that I teach them to you?[50]

CON: You cannot fool me. I am educated about drugs. They are wrong.

PRO: Then why do you assume if you cannot say *no*, you are lacking in moral or educational capacity?

CON: I say no because drugs foster social disruption, violence, and crime.

PRO: Drugs do no such thing. People foster social disruption, violence, and crime.

CON: You are arguing semantics. I will grant you then that people who use drugs foster social disruption, violence, and crime.

PRO: Like the drug-users: George Washington, Thomas Edison, and Sir Isaac Newton I suppose. George Washington, father of social disruptions to Britain. Thomas Edison fierce in his claim to reap the

---

[50] **IDEOLOGICAL AGENTS AS A SUBSTITUTE FOR FAITH**: Regardless of the method of its incorporation into the stream of thought the **ideological agent** must display

- Political stability when it comes into contact with ideologues and other conductors
- A cliché-like simplicity to remain stable in the cisterns of the uneducated
- A warmth of familiarity to refresh the splash pools of youthful imagination
- Low corruption when it comes in contact with plebian logic
- And it must not form too strong a coagulation when imbibed by the fanatical hoards who drink too often from its plentiful waters

But there is more, my friends. If an **ideological agent** is to be really magical, if it is to be truly a savior of a 'way of life', It must make minorities stop acting like minorities and it must lead to a dependency on the social institutions already in place.

rewards of his inventions. And Sir Isaac Newton, the criminal who put God's House in order.

CON: Even if they used drugs, those men were well educated. They are not like the vacuous youth of today, already loose in their citizenship. Preemptive in their social duties. Drugs would only make them worse.

PRO: It sound to me that you cast your vote against education, more so than drugs. For a simple look at electoral statistics will give you the correlation you seek. Those between educational background and voting patterns. Your vacuous youth do not vote. Why then do you fear a change in your electorate?

CON: Our life is a good life. I do not wish it destroyed by drugs or drug-using youth.

PRO: Your life is a leisured life, of this I am assured. But the doctrine by which you live is nothing less than sinister. Under the doctrine of your 'good life': the poor should be motivated by the spur of their poverty; the middleclass motivated by their ability to consume, the wealthy by their incessant accumulation of power, prestige and possessions. And yet, of all these people, who among you ever stops to ask: what do I owe to my education?[51]

---

[51] **WHAT DO WE OWE TO EDUCATION:** Between the sandbox and the coffin there lies a long uncertain period of little recess. And yet, by no means it is clear that early cooperative training on the monkey bars may avert one from a long uncooperative discipline among prison bars. Anymore than it is clear that systematic education may avert one from systematic exploitation.

The cry goes up, "You have the opportunity for education. You have the opportunity to explore ideas. You have the opportunity to find out something about yourselves!" And is this not, after all, the crux of education?

If this is so, then what have we the opportunity to learn from those—who found out very little?

CON: I owe education my social identity[52]

PRO: I am astounded that you can reason so well in this area, yet lack the capacity for reckoning in so many others.

CON: Now it is you—that hears only what you want to hear.

PRO: Perhaps. So I will caution myself. Still, let me not confuse open-mindedness with gullibility. I ask you then, what is it you expect from the educational investment of others?

Especially as it concerns the education about drug-use.[53]

---

[52] **SOCIAL IDENTITY**: a concept of social identity has sought to provide a resolution of our purpose. In short, it concerns itself with our work above mere survival. That is, the works of our religion, our politic, and our economy. And in modern times, a merging of these concepts to form nationalist entities called states, identifiable by their systemic boundaries better known as: Religio-Political-Economies.

For example, America is bounded as a Christian-Democratic-Capitalist state, while Soviet Russia was an Atheistic-Socialist-Collective. The major delinquency in the resolution of these social identities comes when a nation seeks to exploit its logic for unsound purchases. That is, to justify our acts, after the fact, by mixing dogma with tricks of dialectic.

[53] **EDUCATIONAL INVESTMENTS**: A very good question. A question that deserves to be repeated: What exactly is it we expect for our educational investment?

- Better political leaders?
- A change in social performances?
- Greater earning capacity?
- An increase in human capital stores such as skills & knowledge?
- A stronger or gentler society?

Perhaps all these things. Perhaps none. Let us consider. Increased population, expansion of data, compulsory school attendance, increased costs of instruction, the recurrent shortage of teachers, increased needs of better certification for teachers themselves, the injection of machines into the classroom, the bureaucracy of research dominated by corporate concentration, the divided sense of life, the clamor for material abundance, shifts

CON: I assume that education will lead people to examine the principle terms of their social foundation in order to seek to make wise decisions.

PRO: I applaud your assumptions, but let me remind you, even the highest of logical educational forums, that of mathematics, cannot guarantee to make of people—reasonable creatures.

Instead I would suggest you seek how best to tame the basic animal impulses of man. An area of education, that has its own niche in a sub-discipline called behavioral conditioning.[54]

---

in confidence from human to machines, the ambiguous social problems in meaning & authority, and the search for mechanized happiness (that is to say a mechanized freedom from hunger, pain, and even angst), all have affected our educational notions.

Consider that all these things call for a 'technology of teaching'. Not a methodology, mind you, but a technology whose particular mass produced products—students & citizens—can be standardized to fit their generalized target applications.

And yet even as we are driven by the desire for self-direction and self-control, given the hope of freedom from a domination by the past, made cocky by the meanings we attach to our abundant stores of knowledge, and habituated to systematic inquiry, we are hard pressed to see that the difficulties arising in our lives are primarily those we advance through our technologies. To name but three: the generalization of life via mechanization, quantification, and standardization.

Thus we find ourselves staring face to face with something entirely alien to our world—a technological teleology (end-point) of education. Whose end purpose it is reckoned—is to perfect life.

For, after all, who can progress beyond perfection?

[54] **BEHAVIORAL CONDITIONING** attributed to B(urrhus) F(rederic) SKINNER: [1904-1990] a psychologist who looked at humans as programmed automatons to be socially engineered to fit his own version of utopia become Xanadu. See his book *Walden Two* (1948) In the utopia of *Walden Two*, there was no mention of teaching pigeons to pilot torpedoes and bombs, although this is how Burrhus spent his World War II years at the U.S. Office of Scientific Research.

CON: I am all for behavioral conditioning, especially if it will teach our youth not to do drugs.

PRO: Indeed! Then I suspect that you expect all people to conform to conditioning or be sent back to be retooled and honed to a fine finish. Herein the task of every educator would be to condition well-tooled American cogs in educational factories perfectly fitted for a 'democratic' society.

King George, I believe would advocate your conditioning, especially for that free-thinking radical group of folks calling themselves Americans. Whence then the freethinkers beyond America?

Indeed from the earliest times until the present the question uppermost in the minds of authority has been simply: how do we tame the animal impulses of man?

Through proper intellectual conduct, the ancients thought they had discovered means and methods by which to bring man-the-animal under control. And as time passed, the question was given over to the moderns. Yet their means and methods did little more than shift the question from that of *conduct*, to that of *conditioning*.

But in all these times, no one seemed to realize that the really important question is not: how do we tame the animal impulse of man? But rather, How do we tame the impulse of the educated

---

In his book *Beyond Freedom & Dignity* [1971] Burrhus argues that freedom & dignity may lead to self-destruction, and that only a well-disciplined 'behavioral techniques' can save humanity. His air-crib, more commonly known as the skinner box, he invented as a large, soundproof, germfree, air-conditioned baby tender, which he thought could provide the optimal environ for child growth during the first two years of life.

The air-crib is now used, with slight adaptations by pharmaceutical research, for observing how drugs may modify animal behavior; though little attention is given to how the box itself modifies behavior. Say, for example, like the boxes we call—prison or schools in which one can find both 'modifications' and 'pharmaceuticals'.

man? For the birth of ideas itself fathers its own bastard children of intellectual constructions and destructions.

Indeed, it is a measure especially notable in the filtration of ideas down the ranks of educators from social psychologist, sociologists, and other researchers toward the teacher proper. As each has something to say about educational techniques and their efficient use in the process of learning.

But it seems none want to take responsibility for their ideas deleterious effects or failures. Especially when their juvenile ideas are brought back to them by thought-police having discovered them robbing the tombs of great thinkers, and knocking over the gravestones of long dead & virtuous concepts.

And yet, if our intellectual heritage may be said to be an ennobling intimacy with great thinkers of the past, then our intellectual salvation is a hardly more than a lore of great poverty. For who is the disciple of education? And who the pauper? And who is this soul of learning whose robes so worn after many years' usage, flutters by shredded parts loosely hanging? And what of those parts blown away to the clouds?

And so my friend in closing let us turn to the simple question I asked of you earlier: What are the expectations we have created and now hold for Education?

The social scientist, the utopian, the reformer, these people and many others have devoted themselves to the idea of education most simply because they honestly believed that education would make everyone under their tutelage—think like them.

For this reason, education has had a funny way of advancing those of great evil, even as it reduces others of great good. In contradistinction, we find that education may teach us so well, that we learn to reject our political leadership, whose self-indulgent platforms of authoritarian control have grown contrary to our community at large.

Thus I suggest it would be of wise council to devote ourselves to education not because we expect others to be as we, but rather because we believe:

- That certain forms of knowledge enable our understanding while empowering our actions
- That education provides a reference of value by which we can measure ourselves & our efforts
- And that the human image under the guidance of its own education will lead to personal significance

And this includes proper education about drug-use, both casual or otherwise.

Sociological Censorship

Sociological Censorship

Or, a society of censures

PRO: Both George Washington & Thomas Jefferson raised and smoked marijuana.

CON: They did not.

PRO: Their plantation records state otherwise. Therefore we must declare them dope fiends and have their names struck from our sacred history.[55]

CON: Even if I acknowledge the fact that many intelligent people use drugs throughout history, we are not about history alone.

PRO: You are nothing less than the best or worst of history. In a few years your false war on drugs will end as a footnote to war rehabilitation.

---

[55] **MARIJUANA'S AFFINITY FOR PRESIDENTS**: In our own day, we find reports—become nudging jokes—of both president Kennedy and president Clinton, as regards their own elusive run-ins with the demon weed. Though I was unable to locate the references to Jefferson's use of marijuana, the diary of Washington speaks for itself. [See below]

Note that the separation of male & female plants is not necessary for simple cultivation of hemp when it is to be used in products like canvas, clothing, cordage, sailcloth, roping, tarpaulins, twine & yarn; but is beneficial for smoking as the buds of the female plant generally are found more potent.

To read it right from the pen of George himself see his diary entries for the following dates: May 12-13, 1765: *Sowed Hemp at muddy Hole by Swamp*. August 7, 1765:—*began to separate* [sic] *the Male from the Female Hemp at Do- rather too late*.

CON: People don't want rehab. They want drugs.

PRO: Well you promised us a drug-free America and I want mine now. And I want them free.[56]

CON: Legalization will make drugs too available.

PRO: How much more available can we get than in U.S. grade schools and prisons?

CON: Even if they are legal, pushers still will target youth.

PRO: Like wine merchants hang around schoolyards targeting youth, I suppose?

George Washington the Dope Fiend—whatever will Martha think?

As to other references of hemp use in early America, see George Andrews *The Book of Grass: An Anthology of Indian Hemp* [1967] *The Consumers Union Report Licit and illicit Drugs* by Edward M. Brecher & the Editors of Consumer Reports [1972] See Part Ten— *Learning from Mistakes* [521-527], *Policy Issues and Recommendations* [528-539].

For one of innumerable prior historical accounts on the commercial use of hemp I call your attention to the General Court Records at Hartford, Massachusetts [1637] ordering: *every family within this plantation shall procure and plant this present year one spoonful of English hemp seed in some soyle.* [from Mary-Alice F. Rea *Early Introduction of Economic Plants into New England* Econ. Botany 29 (4): pp 333-356

Also see J. Frazier *The Marijuana Farmers, Hemp Cults, and Cultures* 1974 Solar Age Press New Orleans, LA.]

[56] **FREE:** The primary petition is for the legalization of naturally occurring drugs such as coca, marijuana, mushrooms, and peyote.

CON: Ignoring your ridiculous assertion, still, I know the dangers out-weigh the benefits of legalization.[57]

PRO: To say the dangers outweigh the benefits of legalization is a mis-statement of the facts.

CON: It is not, for normal people on drugs behave abnormally. Abnormal people on drugs behave in chilling and horrible ways.

PRO: Normal people on drugs behave normally. Irresponsible people on drugs use drugs as an excuse for their irresponsible acts.

Indeed, I still do not understand why fanatics as you think that inner-city teenage hoodlums are going to act as role-models for middleclass suburbanites; for that is all your argument is really about. You are trying to tell me what you think you know about ghetto stereotypes and their drug-use patterns.

---

[57] **BENEFITS & DANGERS**: The benefits are touted to be:

- Eradication of Black Markets
- Eradication of bootlegging
- Decrease in syndicates which prey on the drug profits
- Collection of tax revenues [over1 billion per year]
- Recovery of enforcement costs [16-18 billion per year]
- Free-up police, judges, courts, time, equipment
- Impure and contaminated drugs taken out of circulation
- Free-up emergency rooms from violence of turf wars
- Decrease in police & political corruption
- Decrease in public cynicism
- Decrease in political prisoners
- increase of rights of privacy
- Decrease of invasions of other countries
- Decrease in the spiking of environment

CON: You can't cure these abusers, middleclass suburbanite or inner-city teen. Every adult who uses drugs already knows the dangers and still elects to use them.

PRO: The dangers are a myth. The user already has heard the rhetoric and propaganda. They do not stop because they know firsthand that you are lying. That's why our kids begin to rebel against authority, they can't stand the hypocrisy.

CON: Drug users are freaks of society. I am defending hardworking honest citizens.

PRO: Drug users are everyday ordinary people. You are hurting hardworking honest citizens who happen to use drugs upon occasion.[58]

CON: No, we are not talking about occasional use; we are talking about vicious gangs high on crack!

PRO: Well while talking about viciousness, please don't forget your vicious drug-enforcement agents sober on fascist power trips.

CON: When the D.E.A suit-up, they're putting their life on the line. Their 'viciousness' to drug traffickers is simply to overcome those who are better trained, better armed, and better financed.

PRO: You've got billion dollar facilities to do nothing more than teach yourselves terrorist methodology under the guise of S.W.A.T. and

---

[58] OCCASIONS: You will note the prohibitionist stereotypes the drug-user as either an Asian or Black gang-member, or as Hippie degenerate contributing nothing to society.

The idea that millions upon millions of middleclass people use casual drugs everyday never seems to occur to opponents of casual drug choice.

Estimates on casual use range from 1-in-8 to 1-in-4. Oddly, in the heat of argument those who oppose drug-use, seem to forget sports heroes, elected clergy, successful actors, prominent politicians, highly decorated policemen, and the scores of successful businessmen who continuously and successfully use drugs like marijuana without any problem, that is, other than those problems of attached stigmas.

you expect me to believe that this training is irrelevant. Now had you told me you simply wish to overlook when the D.E.A. make terrorist raids on casual citizens I would at least grant that you were honest. But hearing this, all I can say is that, at best, all you are—is a big cliché.

CON: Whether I am a cliché is irrelevant, more correctly, we cannot assume people stoned on legal drugs will behave any differently from people stoned on illegal drugs.[59]

PRO: I know we can trust civil people using casual drugs to behave civilly. But more realistically, can we assume drug bigots will behave civilly, once casual drugs are legalized?

CON: Don't mislead the point, drugs are more potent today. The marijuana people smoke today is not the marijuana they smoked in the 1960s.

PRO: Actually, the difference between then and now is that armed raids have forced growers to use better seeds. Thus, all you've told me is that growers are good agriculturalists.

Cities like Amsterdam also sell this more potent weed and drug-related crime is essentially unknown there, because there is no need to control the trade.

---

[59] **STONE SOBER IN AN ANCIENT LAND:** Consider the sober approach of an Arab nation. Here we witness decade after decade the specific extra-ordinary human cruelty perpetrated at every level by people subscribing to an intolerant sober society.

Is it that only the sober are worthy enough to be serviced by the State's redemptions? Or could it be that a purely sober society understands only death, destruction, and hatred for any concept non-soberesque?

CON: Statistics tell me that for users of alcohol, 10% become addicts. For cocaine it is 70%.

PRO: Your statistics lie. The addiction level of which you speak is absurd.[60]

---

[60] **THE QUESTIONS NEVER ASKED OF STATISTICS**: It is quite common, for information-age citizen to make use of personally created statistics in order to make their point, or convince their opponent that they are learned.

Of course, these stats have no basis in reality, no stated source. For example, I got it from *Techno-Farmer's Journal of Bad Seeds*, December issue page twelve, nor any base for reference, for example, per annum use by Polynesian nuns with two left feet between the ages of 24 to 36.

Sadly, when not using self created stats, most of us resort to the dubious testimonial. Dubious because the speaker is obviously attempting to tie their behavior to a specific justification. Moreover dubious because testimonials in no way reflect the behavior of the mass, whether in their purchase of chocolate-covered doughnuts or Ford pintos.

One of the largest fears is that *use* will increase drastically. Of course, *drastically* is a loaded emotional term with no quantifiable state. Moreover, use is of little merit as the behavior is based on consumption. When we consider the alcoholic, note how we do not talk of use but rather of consumption.

Most people who use alcohol never have a problem. And we know that it is the excessive consumption by the individual that is at issue. The same can be easily predicted with the use of casual drugs. The use itself is not a problem, but rather a concern for the few who seek to consume to excess.

As a brief review, recall that covert use is already in place. The numbers presently measure overt use. Total use will not rise by any appreciable degree. For just as a teetotaler was no more likely to use alcohol with the repeal of prohibition, the average citizen is unlikely to use marijuana or other casual drugs once legalized.

Once legal the **covert use** will shift into the **overt use** category and the numbers will reflect an apparent increase. Consumption will also rise as source availability is systematized and brought under quality control guidelines of mass production. A plateau will be reached.

CON: Statistics do not lie. The percentages are correct.[61]

PRO: Indeed it is. In fact, I can tell you something more common and more popular than cocaine—wine.

CON: Again we agree to disagree. Let us take another tack. Prohibition was, after all, a response to a public health crisis.

For marijuana, a conservative estimate is 12% of the adult U.S. population. This corresponds to the popular press use of numbers who contend that there are at least 30 million casual users. Even if we took the lowest and no doubt underestimated governmental figures, that means 1 in 8 people.

Or in different perspective, in a church membership of say 128 people at least 16 of them would use drugs casually without telling the other members.

Additionally, the *National Institute on Drug Abuse* [N.I.D.A.] reports there are 66.5 Americans who experimented with drugs. That is 26.6% of the population. In other words: 1-in-4 Americans.

What then can we expect from all this consumption? Simply this—all products come to market, reach their target plateau and then level off. Eventually the product begins to decline because of substitutes, cultural boredom, or begin to diminish in their personal desires. This fact of business is better known as **market obsolescence**; common knowledge even to the most inept of business people.

Indeed, it is the job of management to apply appropriate campaign strategies for a product based on its current position in the market according to (**a**) incipient, (**b**) growth, or (**c**) decline stage.

In summary, the use argument is selective ignorance at best, black propaganda at worst.

[61] **N.I.D.A.** National Institute on Drug Abuse reports for every addict of crack that there are 33 casual users of cocaine, crack being to cocaine what hard liquor is to beer. Crack made its appearance in the same mode and timeliness as its counterpart hard liquor following the implementation of alcohol sobriety in the 1920s.

The **costs-to-benefit ratio** for running hard liquor versus beer made demon whiskey the drug of choice for the alcohol drug runners. The very same occurred with crack. Cocaine was boiled down into a compact substance and given a new name, **crack**. In short, a concentrated form of cocaine, whose problem of purchase is not knowing how concentrated.

PRO: Prohibition was a response to big business interests.

CON: In whoever's interest it was made, prohibition worked. Per capita alcohol consumption declined. Industrial safety improved, spread of venereal disease slowed.

PRO: Prohibition failed. It was repealed. Overt per capita alcohol consumption declined. Covert per capita alcohol consumption actually increased drastically. Industrial safety was unrelated to prohibition. It was related to work reform.

V.D. decline of which you speak was related to healthcare reforms over the twelve year period that prohibition was in place.

In short, the problems of quality control. This also plagued the prohibition era of demon whiskey.

Following upon World War I, the 1920s prohibition was the direct result of hatred for anything German. Since most of the big brewery owners were of German descent, following the patriotic fervor & unstated bloodlust of World War I, America sucked in its belly, pulled up its zipper, and swore never to piss again. Such Spartan ideals backed up on the social politic creating an America of such hated, bigotry and pretentious righteousness that it was hardly distinguishable from the cesspool of sobriety in which it attempted to wallow.

Our current enforcement of drug sobriety has paralleled that same national folly. It is a direct result of the hatred of Chinese opium use by early California laborers in Chinatown, Orientals, Mexicans & Filipinos, and as well use of marijuana by Blacks linked through stereotypical racism, poverty and cultural disdain.

There were fewer alcoholics, less deaths, less loss of productivity before prohibition than following its implementation. Things returned to pre-prohibition levels several years following repeal. It took some states as long as 30 years to drop their old prohibition laws. And as we know there are still many counties today that remain dry to alcohol sales.

For one popular account of the 1920s see Frederick Lewis Allen *Only Yesterday: an informal history of the nineteen-twenties* Bantam Books 1931

CON: I dismiss your contention. Just as V.D. was a problem to pre-prohibition, thus A.I.D.s is a problem in our times. Most simply I assert legalization will cause A.I.D.s to spread.

PRO: I disagree. Legalization will actually decrease the spread of A.I.D.s.[62]

CON: Obviously on this we agree to disagree. Still it is a fact that drugs hurt, destroy, and inactivate people.

PRO: I will agree that you are wrong, for drugs help, enlighten, and motivate people.

CON: Not so, for not only do drugs hurt, destroy and inactivate, but they also contribute to lost productivity.

PRO: I would suggest you stop trying to fool yourself with such claims. After all, it is Irresponsible workers who contribute to lost productivity, not drugs.[63]

---

[62] **SPREAD OF ARGUMENTS:** The argument runs, decreased prices on legalized drugs will allow users to switch to tablet forms of some drugs now taken by needle.

[63] **LOST PRODUCTIVITY:** facts and figures given for the drug-warring heyday of 1989

- Twice as many people are injured playing golf [68/day] than are treated in emergency rooms from drug-related accidents such as cocaine [37/day]
- There are more people injured using lawn mowers [189/day] than ALL combined drug-related accidents relating to marijuana, cocaine, & heroin

Indeed, there are more people injured

- by chainsaws [153/day]
- by shaving [104/day]
- by bathtub/shower accidents [307/day]
- than drugs of any kind.

CON: It is you who do not see reality, for drugs are responsible for staggering welfare costs.[64]

PRO: Again I must iterate, it is not the use of casual drugs, but simply irresponsible workers.[65]

CON: Children reared by parents that drink are poorly educated and unfit to become part of the intelligent electorate. What then of children reared by parents that use drugs?

PRO: I expect they'll be much less bigoted and much better informed than you.

CON: Our responsibility to ourselves and our posterity is to envision greater possibilities for our society and strive toward those, making

---

SOURCE OF DATA
- Consumer Product Safety Commission
- National Safety Council
- National Institute on Drug Abuse

Or for those less interested in trudging through government reports, might I suggest the quick reference which allows an instant peek at a variety of accidents in life, Tom Heyman's *On an Average Day* Ballantine Publishers 1989

[64] **STAGGERING WELFARE COSTS:** Note how this argument illustrates the want to blame a thing and not the person i.e. to forego holding a person accountable for their acts. *It is the drugs. It is the sugar. It is the diet. It is the upbringing. It is the et cetera.* But never the person.

[65] **IRRESPONSIBLE WORKERS:** As an aside to productivity arguments—by productivity do you think this person means: lost time from work, quality reduction, or that the laborer can't be strapped to the production line for 18 hours at a time?

Consider, cocoa leaves are used by the miners in Brazil just to sustain such large-scale productivity. So I suppose the argument could be made that drugs exploit the workers. Interesting.

whatever sacrifices that are necessary; it must be a society in which our children and grandchildren can live free of the drug curse.[66]

PRO: Our responsibility to ourselves and our posterity is to envision greater possibilities for our society and strive toward whatever sacrifices are necessary. It must be a society in which our children and grandchildren can live free of the drug bigotry.

CON: No one who has seen a crack baby, addicted in the mother's womb could accept the idea that drug abuse is a victimless crime.

PRO: Crack babies are not the result of addicted mothers. They are the result of complex nutritional forces acting together to bring forth underweight babies. You are practicing science without a license to suggest such nonsense.

However in one point you are correct, drug abuse can be devastating. But we are talking about choice for millions beyond the sparse few, who are abusers.

Abusers will always exist of any and every substance. In the old days we called it temperance and spoke of moderation. There are abusers of credit cards. Should we penalize all people for these few? Should we throw the board of Citibank in jail as credit traffickers?

There are people who abuse gasoline—they are called arsonists. Should we shut down every gas station in the nation because a few people kill with gasoline? Should we jail the oil company board members for intent to distribute?

Your argument is criminal in and of itself.

CON: It does not matter. Jail them now. Jail them all.

---

66 **SELF-SACRIFICE:** Even the National Socialists quickly acquiesced on this *making whatever sacrifice is necessary* when they became the targets of state and its new & improved laws, which began to rip their pristine middleclass bodies, belching state slogan bravado, from the comfort of their homes.

PRO: You have done little, but fill our jails with harmless citizens. Citizen who have become nothing more than political prisoners of a new democratic Reich. Abuse is abuse. Based on population averages, abuse neither increases nor decreases. Like all behaviors it has a plateau. Drug abuse, like the abuse of any substance is limited in extent, and you should be ashamed to use such false approaches to attempt to scare and frighten people.

CON: We can't predict the effects of increased consumption that might result from the legalization of drugs.

PRO: Yes we can.

CON: It will get out of control.

PRO: I suppose you mean like wine use is out of control?

CON: Each addict directly affects 4 to 5 other people. This spread will bring about consequences that our society cannot ignore.

PRO: Life is a series of interactions. You cannot fear life. That is all you are doing.

CON: We must not measure the costs in dollars alone.

PRO: You are correct. And we must not measure the costs in fear, folly, and your sober-selected ignorance either.

CON: We must maintain criminal sanctions that persuade people that the good life cannot be reached by dealing drugs.

PRO: I'll be sure to remind my dealer about the lapse in the good life next time we fly to Paris for lunch. By the way, by a good life do you mean freedom from arbitrary search & seizure, freedom from arbitrary wiretaps, freedom from forfeiture of property, freedom from being ostracized?

CON: Drug-use destroys human character. It destroys dignity. It destroys autonomy. It burns away a sense of responsibility. It subverts productivity. It mocks virtue.

PRO: From a more proper view, my panicked friend, it is drug-bigotry that destroys human character; drug-bigotry that destroys dignity; drug-bigotry that destroys autonomy; drug-bigotry that burns away a sense of responsibility; drug-bigotry that subverts productivity; and drug-bigotry that mocks virtue.

If you fail to see what I mean, consider this, drug-use has so destroyed productivity of the drug economy that you cannot find a single laborer, laboratory worker, harvester, driver, or salesmen. Why it has so destroyed drug productivity that even the most sophisticated technological search by the best-equipped sober police force in the world still can't force them to give up their work. Yes. Lot's of lost productivity.

My friend, virtue is but the standard of behavior. And such standards as yours that include bigotry, hatred, and fear against harmless personal choices, are not worth propagating.

CON: I fail to see nothing. Drug-use is wrong.

PRO: Then you truly do miss the basic point, which is: what is wrong with people using casual drugs for leisure, for socialization, for relaxation, good fellowship, or simply for their mind-altering effects?

CON: Because it diverts them from productive work.

PRO: People off work enjoying a beer for leisure, socialization or simply for its mind-altering effects hardly constitute a diversion from productive work. It is their free time to use as they see fit. And likewise with the use of casual drugs.

CON: People can handle beer & wine. But not drugs.

PRO: You're just being foolish now.

CON: Still I believe the use of casual drugs for socialization and leisure is wrong. Why use the artifice of drugs to enjoy life, when you can enjoy life naturally. You can gain the same experience from relationships, from play, from love, & from God.

PRO: You seem to go out of you way to embrace the natural. But were we to listen to your advice we should prohibit books and movies. For neither of these are natural, nor of nature. Nor are these two artificial products gained of relationships, of love, of play, nor of God. They are the artifice of technology.

Indeed, if we were to go through life based only on your false posit of natural experience, we would have to take off our clothes, give up our houses, and abandon our cars. Avoid all medicine & all technologically produced foods.

I believe the use of your argument to be spurious in its naiveté, and childish in its intellectualism.

And yet you haven't even stopped to consider that the drugs we know as coca, marijuana, mushrooms, and peyote, are precisely of nature. And unlike your diet colas, sugar substitutes, manufactured foodstuffs and artificial medicines, not only do these casual drugs add to experience they appositively extend it as well.

CON: The power of drugs on the mind is so severe that the person using them cannot be expected to live up to society's norms.

PRO: That's some incredible psychological legerdemain. You must be a great magician of psychology to negate centuries of men who used drugs on a regular basis and helped to change the world, as we know it.

CON: Let me tell you what I know about famous people who used drugs. What does John Belushi have in common with Elvis Presley, Freddie Prinze, Janis Joplin, Jimi Hendrix, Billie Holiday, Lenny Bruce, and Charlie Parker? They all took drugs. And they all died from doing so.

PRO: Now let me tell you of **renowned individuals who used drugs**. What does Sigmund Freud have in common with Paracelsus, George Washington, Captain Sir Richard Francis Burton, Sir Isaac

Newton, Thomas Edison, Ulysses Grant, Henrik Ibsen, Pope Leo XIII, Emile Zola, Jules Vernes, the Prince of Wales? They all took drugs. And unlike the mediocre entertainment clowns just cited above, their lives and works changed the world as we know it.

CON: In the days of drinking, a man was measured by how much beer he could consume, or by the violence of his acts while inebriated. I do not wish for the rampant use of drugs. For street kids have demonstrated that when they use them, they measure their manliness by how much destruction they can perpetrate.

PRO: In other words, you tell me that by prohibiting the use of drugs, society itself is to blame for removing the social sanctions and rituals that would lead to the self-control and safe-consumption. Very odd reasoning, indeed.

CON: O.K. O.K. Even if I grant that you can handle drugs, and even if I grant the you can learn on them, you, after all, are a special person, much brighter than most, an exceptional individual. Others aren't like you. They will not be able to handle it.

PRO: You sound like a South Afrikaner or Oriental slaver. Them there people can't handle themselves. You can't just give them responsibility. Why, that's Liberty, you're talking 'bout. But 'tis not true, my friend.

It may take some time for readjustment, more for your thoughts than theirs, but to assume that people cannot learn, is to assume they are not fit to rule themselves.

CON: But I'm not willing to take the chance. To lose even one child, is one child too many.

PRO: We're not talking about children. We are talking about adults. And that is an incredibly clumsy way to divert the issue of responsibility. I'd no more allow a child to use drugs, than I'd allow them to drive a car. But I don't mind following your line of reasoning. Let's talk about children for a moment. I would remind you that if you're really that concerned about losing even one child then we must make gasoline illegal.

Too many children have acted as arsonists, and they have killed many innocent people. Indeed, child arsonists have killed more people by their irresponsible acts than any irresponsible drug-user ever has.

In essence the drug-war is little more than typical American laziness. It is premised on the general idea that life is a struggle for limited resources, in this case, limited morals, and limited intelligence. Your drug-bigotry assumes that only non-drug taking and therefore non-alcohol using persons can appositively contribute to society.

Most assuredly, it is easier to appeal to a life whose subjects have ready-made textbooks, instructional materials, and numbered curriculums which champion a hatred for casual drug-users, rather than to question from where the materials are derived.

In short, educational laziness.

CON: If you want to know about laziness, take drugs. For drugs are an escape from the real world.

PRO: Drugs are a part of the real world. Just as you seek to forgive outside the domain of your jurisdiction, you seek to condemn outside the domain of your expertise. Drugs are no more an escape from the real world than are sports, politics, or the nightly tabloid news.

CON: Drugs are a waste of time.

PRO: This conversation is a waste of time; still, I will honor your time with my own. Consider, my friend, the use of the world is a gift. And whatever there is to learn has to be learned in time. But when a person closes their eyes to selected elements of his world, then there is no learning to be had there, in time or otherwise. Your refusal to see the contributive elements of casual drug-use in the world is your loss alone. As much a waste of time, as that wasted by drug-users who see drugs as the whole of their world, ignoring all else.

CON: I tell you again, drugs are a waste of life.

PRO: Your fear of casual drug-use and life is more a reflection of your own inadequacy in the world. You have not lived wisely with your own life and you now project your melancholy on others.

CON: You drug-users are the waste; both of life and of time.

PRO: You should dwell less on the wasted time of others, and see to the vast amounts of time you murder each day.

CON: Every drug addict started out thinking, I can quit when I want to. We must stop the madness, by allowing no one to begin.

PRO: Every casual user started out thinking, why are sober fanatics addicted to irrelevant assertions? Every casual drinker started out thinking; I wonder why the absolute sober fanatics always seek to lecture me based on their obvious perversions counter to the logic of experience?

Like starvation, casual drug-use is entirely remote from your experience. You believe what you choose to believe, and nothing more. You are not interested in facts. Drug use is just another convenient item to pull from the grab bag of generalized excuses concerning areas of life you will never comprehend.[67]

CON: It's not remote. It's about the street, dope, liquor, subsistence whores, a piece of ass, gold chains, and expensive automobiles.

PRO: Now put all that in a movie and show it on a college campus, so they can enjoy it while smoking a joint. Later they can get together to discuss remoteness of experience both philosophically and conveniently over pizza, while they guzzle down that evil dope of yours called economic legerdemain.

---

[67] **LOGIC OF EXPERIENCE:** Indeed, it is difficult to negate experience.

CON: Your mockery does not sway me.

PRO: It seems you cannot truly comprehend what you refuse to experience, whether it is the casual use of drugs or the better use of politics. This is proved in the case of the socialization of beer & wine drinking. And it would be proved in the socialization process of casual drug taking.

Your drug-war is premised on regulation of populations in order to achieve a statistically non-provable solution to maximum economic productivity. You neglect to remember drug-use benefits socialization, improves imagination, and promotes recreational recovery from stress.

Indeed, the whole concept of a drug-war is itself a juvenal dependency and ideological burden. It sterilizes the fertility of imagination, it negates the concept of personal choice, and it replaces the foundations of individual initiative with the unsteady platform of consensual begging after sobriety.

CON: You cannot deny that drug-use leads to dependency.

PRO: Not only can I deny it, I can use it to demonstrate your own narrow-sightedness. The concept of 'dependency structures' is nothing new to the plebian vocabulary or its mundane thought processes.

Dependency structures are borne on the idea that consumption of some resource, in this case casual drugs, personal activity levels, and economic outcomes are directly related and accurately measurable. In this case, the contention is that the drug-user is a dependent on society since they do not participate in productive activity.

For argument's sake let us grant this. Still, we discover that leisure of every kind is a tourism or luxury good for adult consumption based on ability to pay. Thus, the dependent, who has no form of payment can only participate indirectly in the tourism goods of casual drug-use through borrowing, theft, fortuitous finds. However, the drug economy, even though it is currently an underground economy, is still a source of investment capital that maintains its own consumption levels. It maintains its own agriculture, its own harvesting, its own manufacturing, its own storage, its own transport, its own distribution, its own capital formation, its own wage increases, its own policing structures, its own executive salaries.

Like any other economic activity, its investments secure the performance of its active business ventures that work at a profit even in the face of high-risk. Indeed, in the face of high-risk obstacles, it is seen to be not only productive, but fairly timely in delivery of goods, and universally distributed around the globe.

Thus, even the most mediocre of politicians and lawyers should note that this dependency structure is in truth, nothing more than the loser who sits on the couch, perhaps your own Aunt What's-Her-Name. And even if drugs did not exist, Aunt Whozits would still find some excuse for her dependency.

Thus, it is not the actual people associated with the trade, it is not the majority of purchasers who have set aside money for leisure pursuits, but only Aunt Dependency who you pimp as your testimonial.

The problem, of course, is not dependency, but your lazy vision that can only evaluate life based on your own narrow interests.

CON: Drug use compromises the quality of life.

PRO: The use of casual drugs doesn't compromise the quality of life. But a war against casual users certainly compromises numerous lives. The war on drugs is a topic that has diverted attention from other more reasonable goals.

The quality of life is not much aided by your unsupported hysteria and politicized economics. The quality of life would be better if there were fewer of us, but I don't believe this to be a reasonable argument for mass genocide. The fact that you turn the earth into a giant feedlot does not even occur to you.

Instead you occupy your narrow mind with unsupported contentions about casual drug-users.

Please, you must stop all this hated.

CON: The only way I would agree to the legalization of drugs, would be if availably was based solely on I.Q. and racial background.

PRO: I don't think your statement is realistic or morally suitable; much less to say politically viable.

However, such a contention certainly reflects the fact that the drug-war is a political issue that does not reflect the logic of experience; though it does demonstrate its founding on a hatred for other races.

Indeed, even the slow-minded can witness this by examining the following simple observations.

- The stereotype of the drug-user is based on race
- Arrests are judged on economic position[68]
- Interviews & editorials never cover positive aspects of casual drug-use
- Positive role models such as Washington, Newton, & Edison are never mentioned

---

[68] **ECONOMIC POSITION**: For example, famous athletes are put into treatment programs for help with their problem, while the anonymous are put into jail for their crime.

- Activities concerning drugs are organized solely by anti-drug ideologies[69]
- There are no programs or courses at the university level concerning history & sociology of casual drugs
- In seeking guidance, all recommendations are premised on discouragements, not fellowship

---

[69] **ACTIVITIES:** There are no festivals. For example, beer sampling has its October Fest. Wine sampling has its plethora of positive social carnivals. But outside of Amsterdam where is the tasting fair for all the finer varieties of cannabis? Or the competition for improved products, like the finest of wines?

Again, I remind you. There is no need for you to support this state-sanctioned bigotry, hypocrisy, and hatred.

After all, a long training in absurdity will lead you, as its follower, straight toward what its leaders continuously strive to make you remain.

Conspectus

Conspectus

An overall summary of arguments

Since no one has studied the idea of a war on drugs, I have no contemporaries to study. Accordingly, I will offer no historical interpretations. I have presented this collection of arguments so that future historians may have a copula that mediates between juvenile opinions of this historical age and latter hopefully more sophisticated negotiations. Many of these arguments are lame, others undeniably outrageous.

For this there can be no apology. How could there be? These are the thoughts of humans. And though they are expressed by learnéd and modern people, these beliefs expose them as the children they are. Some of these children were in charge of running the nation, others in charge of large corporations. Still other toddlers were persons of the cloth.

May God, science, and our future polity find room to forgive them all.

The history of our drug-war is a history of complementary errors. It may be likened to a German guide-book of France during World War II with its list of possible excursions and leisured repasts once the war has been won. The motive of such guidebooks is clear—it is a motive to encourage its solders to recover from defeat at every turn.

And while such guidebooks to addictive personalities, dysfunctional psychology, and endemic warfare may amuse the more sadistic children of politic or occupy the vague meanderings of the value-neutralized scientists cumma engineers of this age, the twists & turns of the confused participants make little sport upon which the gods may choose to spy.

The modern score has been writ, not as a rule, but as a mood. A sinister chord whose lingering harmony retards thought even as the melody zigzags ahead. Chord into discord, until a strong enough patterns emerge to which every player may dance. And dance they do.

They dance from nooses. They dance through splintered doors. They dance with bullets blown through. Like macabre ballerinas they dance. They dance around the halls of congress, pontificating, plotting, lingering and longing after their shares of the spoils.

Who soiled this area rug of history? We did, of course.

How could we be so cavalier in our comings & goings? Quite simply, it is the same reason, you of our future will be so cavalier, by supposing the world will get better by subscribing to our own peculiar goodness.

Two eras or a thousand away from these days, reasonable souls will come to laugh at our folly. They need not laugh to long or loudly. For the gummy residue of our present will be just as difficult to scrap from the soles of their past.

A few Americans have found their sober ideological quest, the perfect sterility of thought under the guise of a war on drugs.

Let us examine this sterile ideology. For it's salve is scented by both magical cures and selective salvation.

Notes then how the war on drugs assumes all casual users are corrupted equally. It separates family, love, loyalty, and all positive social structures into protectionist policies; while ignoring the fact that casual users likewise demonstrate all of these qualities.

It assumes drugs cause inner-city youth to be as they are. It separates the history of a city's slow decline from casual demonstrations. It never speaks to differences in resource structures within a city. It ignores a city's obsolescence. It ignores decrease in regional competitive ability. It ignores unemployment. It ignores net out migration. It ignores surplus funds of investment pulled from active use. Drug use, and drug-use alone is the problem.

After all, endemic war ideology has always been an exceptionally powerful method of sterile salvation. In the case of our endemic war on drugs it treats casual drug-use as the birth of evil, and ignores that the trade in drugs itself provides schooling, transport, and employment. It keeps the testimonial as its logo, and ignores the fact that experience holds no secrets. It calls casual use bad, and sobriety good. And ignores the fact that they are in all practical terms simply different.

The first aspect you should note about the proponent's arguments is they are never weighted, nor are they ever prioritized.

They are batted back & forth like a tennis ball until the point of the game has been lost. Indeed, that is all this seems to be—a game. A game in which the current state of insouciance [typified male response] and fear [typified female response] encourages the state to perform whatever duties it believes necessary in the spirit of its beaconwords.

Of course, the people involved in these arguments are not attempting to understand any issue. These arguments are simply an alignment with a cause, whether religious, moral, or political. But the "cause" is just the point. For cause too often is foolishly linked to cause-effect. And yet both sides tend to disregard the notion that very few parts of our world are related by simplified arrangements of antecedent cause leading to descendent effect. Indeed, mechanical cause-effect arguments are not applicable to political interactions or social dynamics.

The reality is, since behavior follows no standard cause-effect, no isolated case can escalate. Such persons who seek the claim of cause-effect in the drug domino effect seek no understanding of anything; neither an understanding of self, society, nor people in transition through a historical age.

It would be folly incarnate to tout any of these arguments as fact. For they are nothing more than overt opinions with no basis other than each proponent's ignorance.

Oddly, the CON side of this issue seems at all times more indignant, invective, and righteous in their opinions. It is as though they believe that by throwing their hardened personalities after their offhand thoughts, the rhetorical force might re-align the errant paths and turn them into good arguments—much like a player in a bowling alley as they dance and gesture directions to the ball as it skews off into a gutter.

Policies are judged by their consequences, but crusades are judged by how good they make the crusaders feel.[70]

This statement is brought home most clearly when lawmen jump around like little girls at a pajama party strutting & bragging that they have increased cocaine seizures by 40% in the last decade. It also is quite apparent when the drug salesmen strut & brag that the street price of cocaine has decreased by over 50% in that same period.

In other words, the availability is greater now than it was in the previous 10 years. The fact that the police now have opportunity to seize more, from an even bigger pile doesn't seem to occur to them. But that is to be expected.

For it does not matter that little has been done constructively, but only that the game is in play. And that the players can whack each other on the backside and grin a lot.

The brighter among us already know that societies can not cure every abuser of his/her abuse—whether that abuse involves eating, drinking, or human exploitation. But for some reason the mediocre among us seem to remain ignorant that our falsified ideals can create a community of such brutality and hatred that its realized social conditions do little more than destroy its own citizens.

If nothing else you should realize that as a moral leader you must choose between authentic morality that produces good, and cosmetic morality that merely looks good.[71]

---

[70] **POLICIES ARE JUDGED:** Attributed to Thomas Sowell

[71] **MERELY LOOKS GOOD:** Attributed to John Clifton Marquis, missionary priest assigned to Our Lady of Victory Parish in Compton, CA. from the article *Drugs should be Legalized*

Drug laws look good—but the tragic flaw of is in the cosmetic morality. For like all forms of cosmetics, the change is only superficial and nothing of substance.

Winning—in the case of drug "abuse" for those who might be interested, is finding the direction & methods that provide that maximum amount of health & safety to those who need assistance. Winning is not helping one or two beleaguered souls while turning the rest of society into a monster. [a.k.a. if I can save just 'one' child.][72]

Legalization involves a degree of emphasis, rather than common rhetorical absolutes. Alcohol is certainly legal but it is not legal to drive under the influence. Cocaine & opiates are already legal in that doctors prescribe them. There is a difference between private and public contracts & regulations. It is doubtful that Taco Bell would allow the smoking of marijuana in its facilities any more than it allows cigarette use there.

Drug laws make a mockery of the term free society. For drug-use is a choice not a moral imperative. In short, drug laws are an attempt to legislate sobriety. And toward this end, the sober fanatic's greatest appeal has always been one of hysteria. But hysteria & hypocrisy go hand in hand.

Individual responsibility may be a relic of philosophy and religion but is a sound & necessary relic. The problem with prohibition is that it

---

[72] **SAVING ONE CHILD:** Obviously, or maybe not so obviously, saving one child, while destroying the lives of 100s of others is of no real value. Indeed, it is brutal, callous, and inexcusable.

Teach one child to "Just say no" and "Turn in their friends & family". In turn, we arrest hundreds of parents, take those same children from them, and farm them out to institutional slavery under the auspice of foster care.

Still, this reality of saving one child while in the process of destroying hundreds, does not keep the converts of the *New Therapeutic & Sentimental Love Religions* from making repeated appeals to their own errant acts through this irresponsible vector.

throws responsibility to the wind, in favor, of legalism. But legalism has never been, nor will it ever be, a wise ruler. Legalism, after all, is a tactical force tied to a strategic methodology.

As to a man of wisdom, the last man to rule wisely was Solon, who did so by abdicating his power and leaving the country. Unfortunately, that is unlikely to occur in our own day, for there are none that wise. Nevertheless, and in more serious tone, Prohibition is not drug education, it is intolerance and bigotry.[73]

---

[73] **SOLON:** [630- 560 B.C.] Athenian statesman, known as one of the seven wisest men of Greece. He was Athens' first great poet; but is best known as reformer & legislator, who ended exclusive autocratic control, gave relief to the poor, and introduced Humanitarian Law Code.

Resolution

Resolution to the War

I believe that drug legalization should include the following:

- Coca (rather than cocaine)
- Marijuana
- Mushrooms, &
- Peyote

These are all naturally occurring plants and have been used in a variety of modes by reasoned societies throughout history [spiritually, medicinally, & recreationally]. Tested by time, and without the harmful side effects evoked by most synthetic drugs of technological manufacture.

In any case, legalization should proceed not by changing any current laws, but rather be drawn into effect under a 3 to 5 year period of amnesty. At the end of this trial period, if society deems that the effects are counter to their expectations, the laws would be instantly re-instated without so much as a skip of a heartbeat.

In one scenario, the first set {i.e. coca, marijuana, mushrooms, & peyote} could be set under the amnesty, and after 3 years the others could be fazed onto the list {i.e. cocaine, heroin, LSD, & opium}. At the end of the 5th year, the project would be evaluated and voted on by general assembly. With the laws then being withdrawn from the books. Or in the unlikely event society had yet to mature itself, re-instated.

Such tactics are already utilized in areas as concerns certain forms of illegal behavior such as gambling & prostitution. Where policemen are instructed by their departments just to look the other way. On the rare occasion, things get out of hand; the law is more tightly enforced. Simple. Neat. Efficient.

Again consider the drugs such as: coca, marijuana, mushrooms, & peyote. These plants have been used and are currently being used in religious, social, educational, and recreational formats. Their use is not a problem. The bigotry surrounding them is very much a problem. The attempt to blame a thing such as these drugs as the source for all human ills is not scientific principle—it is quite simply, Dark Age bloodlust. After all, how long do you wish to remain a damn dirty ape?

On Drugs and Education

As to education as a cure-all, I have addressed this posit to a greater degree in a different text, herein I will remind you that the expectation of the lay public laid upon education as universal nostrum is all at once naïve and optimistic. An unrealizable dependence on progress equated with moral growth. For without separating the transmission of cultures from the transmission of knowledge & skills, we humans are apt to believe that behavior [which is culturally dependent] is a matter of timely education [a process independent of culture].

Education about drugs, once it was no longer censured in the class-room, would entail a minimum span of some 16 years of study. Consider such related fields as pharmacology, and then add to that a history of casual drugs, and even the use of nature's drugs in religions. A course of study which is obviously not an instant solution to creating a constituency knowledgeable about drugs and casual drug-use, nor would it be as quick to foster and inculcate artificial opinions, selected ignorance, and specific half-truths though government sanctioned scare tactics under the format of a very thinly disguised social bigotry.

Indeed, proper education requires not only free access to information, testing, and choice but likewise an individual's self-dedication to the pur-suits of mind, moment, and methodology.

Proper education—at least as far as politically charged issues are con-cerned—obviously is not the education that is offered in the classroom. Indeed, the plebian use of the word education has become nothing more than a synonym for social propaganda & control.

In the case of drug education I have witnessed time and again nothing more than same ideological methodology used by the communists, that is,

My children are made to sit as a captive audience while a biased half-informed officer of the state dressed in full uniform indoctrinates him-her interchangeable selves and hopefully others with a well-rehearsed just say nuh-uh lecture concerning the evils of drug losers without a word concerning Washington, Newton or Edison.

This same officer goes out of his-her follow-the-leader way to encourage my children to inform on any parent who according to their bulleted pamphlet's indoctrination rules could be nothing less than a demon-evil incarnate.

But never does Officer Tunnel Vision consider their coffee breaks, tailored uniforms, counter-bored pistols, foreign patrol cars, and badly engineered sweet-treats for Sparky the wonder K-9 whom Officer Lug-Nuts been taught to drag along in order distract the most basic and principle breach of truth is paid for by the self-same evil they propagate.

And God and Government and Science itself will strike dead anyone who dare raise a hand to question the mismanaged budgets of authority.

This hardly constitutes proper education. It does constitute bias, fundamental bigotry, and the opportunistic social politic of propaganda.

But my concern here is not simply with education as it concerns drug-use or drug choice. If this imported communistic become Americanistic (sic) format of indoctrination were isolated in relation solely to casual drug-use, I would be inclined to mumble about prejudice privately [teach my own children how to make their own choices] and leave it at that.

This approach to education, that is this indoctrination, has not defined any boundaries for itself. Indeed, this indoctrination has snaked its way throughout the entire educational process. Enthusiastically conscripted for use in the fostering of all manners of state-sanctioned religious secular humanism and therapeutically assisted pseudo-morality schemes. A platform for religious human worship sanctioned by the same state whose political front spokes models break into a cold sweat at just the mention of teaching the history of religion.

Unfortunately, these state-sanctioned new therapeutic religious programs of reeducation act as if Man is like Sparky—nothing more than a lower animal, who with enough emphasis on control, drill, imitation, obedience, and repetition will somehow magically bring forth creativity, critical decision making, and social freedom leading to truth, justice, and the American Way.

In this case, the American Way has become a vector whose purpose is to raise children ready to be duped by life, irresponsible in their liberty, and careless in their freedom. In all ways, a method which places a high premium on spectatorship and not scholarship. In effect, these programs of reeducation do not lead to freedom or justice. Or even more simply—to creativity or truth.

Indeed, the result of such state-sanctioned therapeutic indoctrination is a program that fosters the very insouciance it was created to battle. In other words, it is a public lesson that demonstrates that oppression is a valid method of governance as long as it can be enforced. A lesson that demonstrates that the really valuable tools of society are—bigotry in the majority, weapons of enforcement, & coercive techniques of indoctrination.

Is it any wonder then that our brighter children begin to wonder why they should remain attached year after year to a classroom where they have become nothing more than unwilling props in a theatre of the absurd?

True drug legalization encompasses many positive aspects of our social life. When drug choice is returned to the citizens of the United States, the least likely will find that they are more aspects to be dealt with than the simplistic childhood ranting & raving of drug bigots.

On Drugs & Recreation

No matter how persistent the persecution, no matter how severe the punishment, no matter how great the suffering, and no matter how vile the threat of recrimination by sober fanaticism, the reality of experience can never be negated.

The margins of the primitive mind are sustained by fear and prejudice, not what is experienced or known. The fear of casual drugs is a fear unsound. A childish projection of soberists trained to compliance, not to understand. The diminished power of the fanatically sober is maintained by absolute necessity. The necessity to remain fixed in the mundane. It is an endeavor taught to persons from birth, by a culture which does not value their capacity, and which does not support their creativity, but rather wishes to harness their labor for the good of the hive.

Perhaps I am the last in this era to learn from history, philosophy, and theology that the impetus, growth, and increase in human capacity comes from outside the rigid structure of enslavement to tradition—whether that enslavement be spiritual, mental, or cultural in nature.

Indeed, the society that does not value capacity becomes a technology. Experience teaches us that there is fertility of illumination in drug surrogacy; of this there can be no doubt.

And yet, I am aware that there exists large-scale frivolous use of drugs, whose purpose is not to be cognizant of health, education, and freedom. Whose style of drug-use is as frivolous as their poetry, music, & politic.

But to those people, I must declare: the return on your investment in the casual use of drugs use is obtained by focus and clarity of purpose.

Consider the mundane case of the sober fanatic who spends vast amounts of their day in frivolous, ephemeral pursuits. And yet no one accuses you of killing time or staying soberly high. And yet your sober poverty and its attendant disequilibria are directly responsible for productivity declines, criminal activity, and wasted lives. Indeed, the poverty of the sober bigot leads again & again toward trite dreams of thoughtless consciousness.

So it is understandable that the plebian mind that engages drugs in the same manner of the trite and provincial thought of a sober idiot will likewise carry forward this same inertia into the casual drug experience. And once the orientation begins to encompass them, they focus more & more on allowing their feelings to override their responsibility, than on the experience toward a better control. They have learned not in sobriety how to center, focus, or contemplate. Thus, it is not likely they will learn while attempting to further distract themselves.

Still, they can learn.

I do not discourage, nor encourage such banal activity as recreational drug-use, but it should be clear that this is, after all, recreational use and not educational use. Thus, no one wise should be surprised to find that all drug-related studies to date have produced findings & summaries that are as inane as investigating the spurious life of the sober fanatic.

Imagine the same D.A.R.E. nonsense targeted against the lazy & the indolent who bob & weave through their day & nights in pursuit of nothing more than television programming. What do you think such studies would reveal beyond self-imposed ineptitude?

In any account, I hold that the banal use of time whether under the sober-experience or the drug-experience must be and are without excuse accountable in full and to the same degree for all acts: good, bad or bland. I state that all acts under the influence of drugs or under the influence of sobriety are the individual's and the individual's alone. Each of us is entirely responsible for own acts both on and off drugs at all times.

In short, there is no authority without accountability.

A Summary of the Arguments

Once you remove the diplomatic niceties and tone down the bigotry, the overview goes something like this:

Since people put smoke into their lungs,

War metaphor says: let's kill leaders, plants, and users. Change our banking structure and money. Enlist more men, money, time, effort, & propaganda. Change our laws. And invade any country necessary because we're fighting for hearts & minds. It's encouraging even in our sober floundering.

Counter-arguments to war say: it is insane. More men, money, time, effort, & propaganda are not going to help, even if we waste all these resources over another lifetime of our wondering attention spans. We would like to have our Bill of Rights back in tact. And we can still invade countries over oil or bananas.

Business arguments say: other countries will make more money than us. Spin-off markets & new products will hurt our people while decreasing our productivity.

Counter-arguments say: capitalism is about money & the plateau of sales/purchases is limited. Spin-offs & new products are welcome. Productivity will increase by new ventures, additional jobs, and exports.

Moral metaphor says: people are ruthless. Drugs are evil—even Satan won't use them. Everyone will be inebriated all the time. All our babies will be stabbed & eaten alive on the steps of the church by drug crazed gang members with Uzi's and Nike clown shoes.

Counter-arguments say: by these laws we have become the ruthless & evil ones. Insobriety is insignificant [like purchases they remind us that abuse is a small plateau] and limited in scope. Government officials are stealing our homes, property, & children and auctioning them off to the public and to the vagaries of institutionalized foster care. Bigotry, hatred, & unrealistic fears—not drugs—are the problem.

Rights arguments say: it's a good law.

Counter-arguments say: Bill of Rights (amendments 4, 5, & 8) has been usurped.

Social arguments say: legalization will increase—crime, gangs, violence, & trash on our highways—because all life is a domino effect. Life is good & we are scared of the future. We hate those kind of people. Drugs are the ultimate demon evil & bad for your health. And it will corrupt our youth, clergy, and show people.

Counter-arguments say: bigotry would remind us that. dominos in their natural state [i.e. laid flat] do not fall over. We are the one's hurting the environment [runoff from spiking plant life], hurting the innocent & casual users & their children, destroying our motivation, morale, & spirit, and making a mockery of this nation's potential. No matter how many police & politicians corrupt themselves, plenty of wonderful historical figures and personable heroes have used drugs, and like the majority of us never had a problem. We would benefit by the extra income {tax (1 billion), peace dividend (16-18 billion), government restructuring, D.E.A. restructuring, and fines for misbehavior). Besides our health is fine.

And finally, the priorities indicate:

- **Abuse use** is statistically insignificant.

- **Teen use** will decline to insignificance once legal.

- **Misbehavior** will be fined.

- **Business transactions** will offer growth potential.

- **Mere use** is unimportant.

Bibliography

Bibliography

- AUTHORS, general

- AUTHORS, conceptual

- AUTHORS, specific ◀ **main index**

- EDITED WORKS

- REFERENCE WORKS, councils & commissions

- REFERENCE WORKS, general

- RELIGIOUS WORKS

- TRANSLATED WORKS

Bibliography Legend

Main INDEX: The main index is called **AUTHORS, specific.** It lists all books cited, in the main text, as well as those consulted in the course of this treatise. It also cites books placed under their own headings, that is, under sections such as the Edited, Religious, & Translated Works.

Bold FACE: In the main index, you will find certain author's names appear in boldface. These books indicate a formulation of worldviews which in and of themselves you may find of Interest.

NORMALIZED: Books marked with a 1° are of primary importance to this work. Books marked with a 2° are secondary in importance, and those marked 3° are tertiary. All others are of but casual reference. This normalizes the use of works cited.

Publish DATE: Except for the last section, all sections are arranged in an alpha list by authors' last names. If the publication date is uncertain or unknown it will appear to the closet known units.

> For example—188x indicates the publication lies between 1880 to 1889. Likewise, a publication may be only vaguely given as *circa 465-433 B.C.E* because its authorization is uncertain, or, it has been edited over time by a variety of persons.

Use of Page Numbers

Page NUMBERS: Throughout the text references to page numbers are given as a number followed by a letter. For example, **101a.** This would indicate page 101, paragraph a. The letter simply designates the paragraph starting from the top of that page. This noted, I now draw your attention to special use of the letters { **A**, **a**, **ß**, and multiple letters }.

If the paragraph is at the **top of the page** it would be indicated by:

> **101A** indicates full paragraph at top of page 101
> **101a** indicates partial paragraph at top of page 101

If the paragraph is at the **bottom of the page**, it would be indicated as:

> **102ß** indicates where *Beta* indicates bottom of page 102

If the paragraph appeared in the second column in the fourth paragraph it would be indicated as

> **103dd** indicates second column, fourth paragraph, on page 103

Or if the paragraph was in the third column in the second paragraph:

> **104bbb** indicates third column, second paragraph, on page 104

AUTHORS, General

This section contains a list of persons whose works and ideas were consulted in the course of this treatise. It does not list any books, but rather describes in what regard they were consulted.

• A

Ambrose: Saint Ambrose, Bishop of Milan—in regard to chastisement of the Christian Emperor Theodosius I

Aristotle : Aristotle, Greek educator & philosopher—in regard to slavery being a natural state for some men; & ends of cause (matter, agent, plan, purpose). Compare Ends of Cause with (mass, momentum, pattern, intent).

Arras : Betty Arras, editor & journalist—in regard to her publication California Monitor of Education

Aquinas : Thomas Aquinas [Italian Tommaso d'Aquino] Italian religious commentator & philosopher—in regard to his concept of venial sin, scholasticism, & the reformation

Averroës : Averroës, Islamic Spaniard, philosopher & physician—in regard to his commentated translations of the ancients—Plato, & Aristotle

• B

Barberini : Maffeo Barberini, Pope Urban Viii—in regard to his prosecution of his friend Galileo

Baum : Frank L. Baum, writer—in regard to his children's books *The Wizard of Oz & The Return to Oz* series as an example of fairytale (vs.) myth

Bodin : Jean Bodin, economist—in regard to development of economic theory

Brouwer : L. E. J. Brouwer, mathematician—mentioned in regard to topology

• C

Calvin : John Calvin, French theologian—in regard to theological subversion

Charles : Charles, prince of Wales, heir to the throne of England—in regard to mercenary armies as world police

Clausewitz : Carl von Clausewitz, Prussian general—in regard to political subversion

Copernicus : Nicolaus Copernicus [in polish—Mikolaj Kopernik], astronomer—in regard to his re orientation of planetary motion around the Sun rather than the Earth

• D

Descarte : René Descarte, French mathematician & philosopher—in regard to mapping between elemental sets

Donohue: Phil Donohue, talkshow host—in regard to The Donohue show's use of unreliable stats, as teleprophets in general, political aggrandizement, & the frequent quote—'you're good, you're smart, you're bright', ad naseum

• E

Einstein : Albert Einstein, German physicist—in regard to his Theory of Relativity conscripted for use in the soft sciences

Eve: Eve, mate of Adam—in regard to temptress through which evil entered the world

• F

Farrakhan : Louis Farrakhan, religious Leader—in regard to his transition from political religionist to psycho-political amalgam

• G

Galliani : Abbé Galliani, historian—in regard to Fall of Rome as less a fall than a transition from Roman to German landlords

Gandhi : Mohandas Karamchand Gandhi, Indian lawyer & social reformer—in regard to his philosophy of Ends & Means

Goya : Francisco José de Goya y Lucientes, Spanish painter—in regard to The Dream of Reason breeds Monsters

Grotius : Hugo Grotius, [MORE at 'Huigh de Groot'] Dutch jurist & statesman—in regard to his comment, 'Natural Law is so immutable that God himself can not change it.'

• H

Hawthorne : Nathaniel Hawthorne, writer—in regard to the damned female scribblers

Heidegger : Martin Heidegger, German philosopher—in regard to German Philosophy & Ideology

Hilbert : David Hilbert, German mathematician—in regard to Set Theory

Hitler : Adolf Hitler, German chancellor and fuehrer—in regard to his eugenic experiment on German Culture

Hussein : Saddam al-Tikriti Hussein, Iraq dictator—in regard to Sobriety, & the Credo—'Benevolence to the People, Violence to the Enemy of the People'

• I

Isocrates : Isocrates [436-338 B.C.E], Athenian orator—in regard to early schools of philosophy & education

• J

Jackson : Jessie Jackson, religious leader—in regard to Black Laws of Mind

Jeanne : Jenne d'Arc [in America Joan of Arc], the Maid of Orleans & French national Heroine—in regard to Galileo as male version

Jefferson: Thomas Jefferson, 3rd president of the U. S.—in regard to poetic justice

Jesus: Jesus, religious Leader—mentioned in regard to ethical self-reflection; denial as the King of Kings; & Search for the highest level of humanity

Jones : Jim Jones, religious leader who lead his congregation to mass suicide—in regard to the Church vs. the State

Joyce : James Augustine Joyce, Irish writer—in regard to his novel Finnegans Wake

• K

Kant : Immanuel Kant, German philosopher—in regard to formalizing subjectivity

Karresh : David Karresh, religious leader who lead his congregation to mass suicide—in regard to Church vs. the State

King : Martin Luther King, clergyman & social reformer—in regard to his oft touted speech, 'I have a Dream …'

Koop : C. Everett Koop, physician—in regard to utilizing the Office of Surgeon General as a platform for state sanctioned 'truths'

• L

Lilith: Lilith, 1st mate of Adam—in regard to her 'demonic' offspring

Lister : Joseph Lister, English surgeon—in regard to his Introduction of antisepsis via the use of carbolic acid in surgical performances

Locke : John Locke, English philosopher—in regard to his views on education

Luther : Martin Luther, German theologian—in regard to his warning about a Cult of Reason

• M

Machiavelli : Niccoló Machiavelli, Italian political philosopher—in regard to development of economic theory

Malthus : Thomas Robert Malthus, English economist—in regard to population theories

Marquis : John Clifton Marquis, missionary priest—in regard to moral leadership

Marx & Engels : Karl Marx & Friedrich Engels, sociologists—in regard to feminist conscription of political rhetoric

Marx : Karl Marx, German political philosopher—in regard to philosophical subversion; & in regard to his philosophy & ideology

Mendal : Johann Gregor Mendal, Austrian educator & monk—in regard to his postulations concerning independent assortment

Merlin : Merlin [MORE at 'Myrddin'], a prophet and mage in Arthurian Legend—in regard to psychiatry as Mage to the Court of Absurdity

Moltke : Helmuth von Moltke, Prussian general—in regard to the essence of successful war making

Mun : Thomus Mun, English economist—in regard to development of economic theory

Murrow : Edward R. Murrow, journalist—in regard to his documentary—*Harvest of Shame*

• N

Newton : Isaac Newton, English physicist—in regard to his 2nd law of force

Nietzsche : Friedrich Wilhelm Nietzsche, German philosopher—in regard to Atheism

• P

Parmenides : Parmenides, Greek philosopher circa 515 B.C.E.—in regard to originator of the fundamental problems of metaphysics

Pavlov : Ivan P. Pavlov, Russian physiologist—in regard to dog saliva, response of the therapeutics, & transference of childhood

Popper : Karl R. Popper, German mathematician & philosopher—in regard to Growth of Knowledge and the Logic of Scientific Discovery

Ptolemy : Claudius Ptolemaeus, Alexandrian astronomer circa 2nd Century A.D.—in regard to his refined circles within circles to explain the motion of the planets about the earth

Proudhon : Pierre-Joseph Proudhon, French journalist—in regard to population theories

• Q

Quesnay : François Quesnay, French physician—in regard to development of economic theory

• R

Reagan : Ronald Reagan, 41st president of U. S.—in regard to innocuous questions; & puppet kings

Roberts : Oral Roberts, religious Leader—in regard to the wraith of his Great Maker

Robertson : H. M. Robertson, historian—who stressed the Jesuits behind 'capitalistic economies'

• S

Schleiermacher : Friedrich Schleiermacher, German philosopher—in regard to the tendency/need to divide understanding between the subjective and objective

Schopenhauer : Arthur Schopenhauer, German philosopher—in regard to concept of Spirit as Will; & in regard to philosophical answers to desperation

Serra : Antonio Serra, economist—in regard to development of economic theory

Shiller : Johann Christoph Friedrich von Shiller, poet & dramatist—in regard to German literary movement

Smith : Joseph Smith, religious leader—in regard to his Revelations leading to the Founding of the Church of Latter Day Saints [a.k.a. Mormonism]

Solon : Solon, Athenian statesman circa 550 B.C.E.—in regard to legislation & reform

Sombart : Werner Sombart, historian—who stressed the Catholic Loyalists as impetus behind capitalism

Sophocles : Sophocles, Greek dramatist—in regard to his expression 'One can not pass judgment on the life of mortals and say if it has been happy or unhappy until their death.'

Sowell : Thomas Sowell, author—in regard to policies as crusades

Spencer : Herbert Spencer, English philosopher—in regard to categorization of man

Spengler : Oswald Spengler, German philosopher—mentioned as historian of cultural morphology

Stearn : Howard Stearn, disk jockey—in regard to nontraditional agendas & selected persecution by the State

• T

Tawney : R. H. Tawney, English economic historian—who stressed the role of Jews as the Impetus behind capitalism

Thorndike : E. L. Thorndike, psychologist—in regard to Social Darwinism

• V

Vico : Giambattista Vico, Italian philosopher—mentioned in general as a Philosopher of History

Voltaire : François-Marie Arouet, French writer—in regard to social commentary

• W

Washington : Booker T(aliaferro) Washington, educator—in regard to industrial training vs. classical formats of education directed toward Negroes during first common school reform

Washington : George Washington, solder & president—in regard to his diary entries dated May 12-13, 1765; & August 7, 1765

Winkle : Rip Van Winkle, fictional hero—in regard to pantyhose Lectures, petticoat tyranny, and dreams of escape from the shrew

Winfrey : Oprah Winfrey, talkshow host—in regard to the Oprah Winfrey Show's use of unreliable stats, as teleprophet in general, 'Lack of WILL', 'save the world', etc ad naseum

AUTHORS, Conceptual

This section contains a list of authors whose concepts are similar enough in nature to regard in a common framework. This section does not list any books, but rather describes in what regard these authors were consulted.

Concept Set : Adam Smith, John Stuart Mill, Knut Wicksell, Irving Fisher, Hyman Minsky—and the economic posit of 'overtrading' leading to cyclic crashes

Concept Set : Adam, Eve, Serpent—in regard to the World Tree, & Fall from Grace

Concept Set : Adam, the Nation of Israel, Jesus—in regard to a unified [Christian] spiritual history

Concept Set : Amos, Isaiah, Marx, Mohammed, Nietzsche, Hegel, Wordsworth, Thomas Aquinas, Schopenhauer, Augustine, Freud—in regard to ideas of God

Concept Set : Aristotle, King James II, Massachusetts Governor Edmund Andeos—in regard to Mather family

Concept Set : Aristotle, Montesquieu, Hume—in regard to political theorists

Concept Set : Aristotle, Newton, Einstein, Darwin/Lyell—in regard to world perspective changes & the decline of Christianity

Concept Set : August Comte, Immanuel Kant—in regard to Unity of Knowledge

Concept Set : Augustine, Thomas Aquinas, Scholastics—in regard to contemplative vs. speculative philosophy

Concept Set : Averroës, Aristotle, Maimonides—in regard to Faith vs. Reason

Concept Set : Bazaar, Cosmo, Ebony, People, Time—a Variety of Magazines—in regard to being the descendents of moralizing 'news accounts'

Concept Set : Beats, Black Panthers, Bohemians, Hippies, Women's Libbers, Yippies, etc—in regard to education as a counter to 'revolutions' and therefore as a social stabilizer

Concept Set : Bohr, de Broglie, Einstein, Heisenberg, Plank, Schrödinger, et Al—in regard to the thirty years [1900-1930] leading to the synthesis of a variety of paradoxes in physics

Concept Set : Buddhism, Christianity, Islam—in regard to blended amalgams of moral perfection

Concept Set : Cargo Cults of Melanesia—in regard to Synchronistic Religious Movements, & Pagan Intellectualism. Compare with the Papuan Vailala Madness in 1919. And note how the New Therapeutic & Sentimental Love Religions in our own day via their motto 'the highest level of humanity' seek to reassert the expression of Christian traditional millennial ideas, as a revival/transmutation of eschatological (a.k.a. 'End of the World') teachings encouraged by massive material wealth interpreted as coming from technological (a.k.a. 'supernatural') sources beyond their ken. In essence, the converts to the New Therapeutic & Sentimental Love Religions have begun to prepare themselves for a 'radically new age', thought to be inaugurated by events that will destroy the old order, and bring paradise via freedom & justice. And note how few, if any, commentators have given consideration to the enormous waste of economic and political energies connected with this mass movement, much less its implications.

Concept Set : Charles Darwin, Charles Lyell, Benjamin Franklin, Josiah Nott—in regard to evolution

Concept Set : Chaucer, Milton, Shakspeare (sic)—in regard to the standard format of classical English literature

Concept Set : Christianity, Judaism, Islam, Buddhism, Confucius, Taoism—in regard to revelations

Concept Set : Chuang Tzu [literally Master Chuang], Mumon—in regard to The Tao

Concept Set : Copernicus, Ptolemy, Luther, Calvin, Jesuits—in regard to the effects of 'scientific reasoning' on historians

Concept Set : Dante, Newton, Gauss, Lobachevsky, Washington, Lincoln—in regard to satisfaction of progress

Concept Set : Darwin, Lyell—in regard to the habits of trained reason

Concept Set : Darwin, Lyell, Newton, Einstein—in regard to the limits of the metaphors of science

Concept Set : Defoe, Fielding, Richardson—in regard to the rise of the 'novel'

Concept Set : Dependents of Science, Worshipers of Therapy, faithful human Secularists—in regard to 'unnumbered' appeals to statistics. ['unnumbered' compare 'unlettered'.]

Concept Set : Descarte, Galileo, Francis Bacon—in regard to the co-founders of the methodologies of science

Concept Set : Descarte, Galileo, Francis Bacon—in regard to the logical faith in 'experimental reasoning'

Concept Set : Eranos Circle {Carl Jung, Mircea Eliade, Karl Keréyi}, Erich Fromm—in regard to contributions to history of religion

Concept Set : Francis Bacon, Descarte, Galileo—in regard to transmutation of ineffable faith into formalized faith leading to scientific methodology. That is, from **faith** to **doxy** (opinion), to **heterodoxy**, to **orthodoxy**, to **doctrine** into **dogma**

Concept Set : Freud, Jung, Skinner, Sullivan, Ernest Borgnine—in regard to subscription philosophies

Concept Set : Freud, Lister—in regard to the habits of surgeons, septic and antiseptic

Concept Set : Friedrich Herbart, Friedrich Froebel, John Dewey, Paul Goodman—in regard to various schools of educational philosophy

Concept Set : Giambattista Vico, Oswald Spengler, Arnold J. Toynbee—in regard to the posit of historical phases/cycles

Concept Set : Herbert Spencer, T. H. Huxley—in regard to the first apostles of a culture of science [See the works of these authors cited in the main index above.]

Concept Set : Hitler, Stalin, Mao Tse Tung—in regard to 'working for the good of humanity'

Concept Set : Hohenzollern Dynasty, Frederick William I, Frederick II—in regard to the origin of the abstract entity called the—State

Concept Set : Homer, Stoics, Greeks—in regard to historian J. B. Bury's comment on the notion of human progress

Concept Set : Huguenots of France, Lutherans, Calvinists—in regard to the Thirty Years War [ended 1648] which won for the Mother Church the suppression of exegetical commentary. (Critical interpretation of a text)

Concept Set : Huguenots, Exegetical Commentaries of the Protestants—in regard to the effects of 'scientific reasoning' on religionists/theologians

Concept Set : Humanistic Scholarship—in regard to the 'highest levels of humanity'

Concept Set : Islam, Judaism, Oriental Religions—in regard to change in the center of time [from BC/AD to BCE/CE]

Concept Set : Jesus, Gandhi, Buddha—in regard to violence begets violence, though peace may not beget peace

Concept Set : John Locke, David Hume, Immanuel Kant—in regard to metaphysics

Concept Set : K.K.K, Grand Uncle Titan of the Invisible Empire of the Ku Klux Klan—in regard to self-sustained evil, hate, terror, etc

Concept Set : K.K.K, 'Nation' of Islam—in regard to sacrificing [appositive] creativity, evading truth, and usurping individual capacity, for self-indulgent failure and sickness

Concept Set : Kant, Descarte, Hobbes, Berkeley, Schopenhauer, William James—in regard to Unity of Reality

Concept Set : M. Scott Peck, Oprah Winfrey—in regard to conflict resolution

Concept Set : Mark Twain, Herman Melville, James Fenimore Cooper, Stephan Crane, Edgar Allan Poe—in regard to the American novel's crossover into children's literature.

Concept Set : Marx & Engels, Chauvin, Feminists—in regard to the pirating of Marxist rhetoric by the Feminists. [NOTE: Nicolas Chauvin is a character noted for his excessive patriotism and devotion to Napoleon. He appears in the play *La Cocarde Tricolore* (1831) written by Théodore and Hippolyte Cogniard. Compare *Chauvinism* to—*Jingoism*.]

Concept Set : McCarthy Hearings, Douglas Ginsberg Hearings, drug Tsar William Bennett, National Socialists—in regard to climates of persecution

Concept Set : Mohammed, Marques de Sade—in regard to archetype unifications

Concept Set : Monty Python, Czech Directors—in regard to Münchausen, Teller of Tall Tales

Concept Set : N. Bourbaki, Julian Jaynes, Derek Bickerton—in regard to the standardization of concepts. And note that N. Bourbaki (a.k.a. Nicolas Bourbaki) is not a person, but rather a group of mathematicians who publish their theories under this pseudonym. Beginning in 1939 with their first Volume *Éléments de Mathématique* [translation: *Elements of Mathematics*] by 1974 they had produced over 36 volumes. The actual membership remains secret though it is known that the group is ever-changing.

Concept Set : Oprah Winfrey, Marianne Williamson—in regard to Synchronistic Religious Movements, Pagan Intellectualism, and perceptions which remain rational only within their own worldview

Concept Set : Patriarchs, Jesus, Oral Roberts, Jim & Tammy Baker, Billy Graham—in regard to 'Living Laws'

Concept Set : Philosophers of the Manifold, Philosophers of the Process—in regard to time

Concept Set : Plato, Augustine, More, Bacon, B. F. Skinner, Paul Goodman—in regard to Utopia(s)

Concept Set : Plato, Marx—in regard to their speculations on social order

Concept Set : Plato, Marx, IRS—in regard to the classification of people in society

Concept Set : Plato, Marx, IRS, Skinner—in regard to Utopian administrations

Concept Set : Popes, Bishops, Jesus—in regard to 'faith in all males' denied

Concept Set : Pythagoras, Empedocles, Buddha—in regard to cycles of birth-destruction-rebirth

Concept Set : Richard, Increase, & Cotton Mather—in regard to this prominent family of early New England

Concept Set : Richardson, Marivaux, Prévost, Goya—in regard to attacks on Reason [a.k.a. 'Rationalism'] by the romance writers and artists [a.k.a. the 'Romantics']

Concept Set : Schizophrenics, Paranoids, & Neurotics—in regard to words applicable to their founders

Concept Set : Sigmund Freud, Carl Jung, Adolf Bastion—in regard to archetype formulations

Concept Set : Social Scientists, Empiricists, Educator, Man in general—in regard to educational expectations

Concept Set : Social Scientists, Utopians, Reformers, etc—in regard to education as a method of control

Concept Set : Sophists, Plato, Isocrates—in regard to 'ethical-political' education [i.e. to train talented youth for political leadership]

Concept Set : St Augustine, Kant, Hegel, Marx, Spengler, Toynbee, Ellul—in regard to historical unity

Concept Set : Surrealists, Marxists—in regard to altering the conventions by which we examine the world

Concept Set : The Huxley Family (vs.) the Kennedy Family—in regard to multigenerational families and their effects on history

Concept Set : the Kennedy & Johnson Administrations—in regard to the 'War on Poverty'

Concept Set : Traditionalists, Therapeutics, Scientists, Educationalists, Politicians, Classes—in regard to contrary requirements for 'basic' educational foundations

Concept Set : Washington Irving, Caesar, Adam Smith, Aristotle, Abraham Lincoln, Andy Mellon, B. J. Palmer, etc—in regard to quote by H. L. Menken concerning the education of the poor

Concept Set : Wheeler, Jaynes—in regard to unconscious metaphorical treatments of Kant's earlier formulations

AUTHORS, Specific

THIS IS THE MAIN INDEX. It lists the authors and their works which were consulted during the course of writing this treatise. As previously stated, the books which appear below marked 1° are of primary importance to this work. Books marked 2° are secondary in importance, and those marked 3° are tertiary. All others are of but casual reference. This normalizes the use of works cited.

• A

Abbott : Martin Abbott *Freedmen's Bureau in South Carolina*

Abro : See below—d'Abro.

Adams : John Adams [1735-1826] *Defense of the Constitution of Government of the U.S. of America* 1787

Adler : Mortimer J. Adler *The Four Dimensions of Philosophy* [those dimensions being—metaphysical, moral, objective, categorical] 1993

Adrian : E. Adrian (et AL), editor *Brain Mechanisms and Consciousness* [collection of articles] 1954

Albert & Denise & Peterfreund : Ethel M. Albert, Theodore C. Denise, Sheldon P. Peterfreund *Great Traditions in Ethics* [fourth edition] 1980

Alcott : William A. Alcott *Young Man's Guide* 1833

Alexander & Selesnick : Franz G. Alexander, & Sheldon T. Selesnick *The History of Psychiatry: an evaluation of psychiatric thought and practice from prehistoric times to the present* [MORE at till 1966] 1966

al-Khalil : See below—Khalil.

Allen : Frederick Lewis Allen *Only Yesterday: an informal history of the nineteen-twenties* 1931

Allen : William Sheridan Allen *The Nazi Seizure of Power: the experience of a single German town 1930..1935* 1973

1° **Altieri** : Charles Altieri *Act & Quality: a theory of literary meaning and humanistic understanding* 1981

Althoen & Bumcrot : Steven C. Althoen & Robert J. Bumcrot *Finite Mathematics* [in regard to math illiteracy] 1976

Amadeus : See below—Mozart.

Andrews : George Andrews *The Book of Grass: An Anthology of Indian Hemp* 1967

Aristotle : Aristotle *Poetics* [translation by S. H. Butcher] retiled—*Aristotle's Theory of Poetry & fine Art* 1951

Aristotle : Aristotle *Metaphysics* [translated by Hippocrates G. Apostle, includes *Commentaries* 1966 (1979)]

Aristotle : Aristotle *Physics* [translated by Hippocrates G. Apostle, includes *Commentaries* 1969 (1980)]

3° Armstrong : Karen Armstrong *History of GOD: the 4000 year quest of Judaism, Christianity, and Islam* 1993

Arras : Betty Arras *The California Monitor of Education* [publication]

Arthur : Timothy Arthur *Ten Nights in a Bar-Room* [fiction] 1854

Augustine : St. Augustine [354-430] *The City of GOD* [circa 396 A.D.]

• B

1° **Bach** : Maurice J. Bach *The Design of the Unix Operating System* [a text —in regard to 'systems' in general] 1986

Bacon : Francis Bacon [1561-1626] *Essays* 1597/1612/1625 [most specifically the Essays **1**—of Truth; **3**—of Unity in Religion; **10**—of Love; **13**—of Goodness, and Goodness of Nature; **16**—of Atheism; **23**—of Wisdom for a Man's Self; **38**—of Nature in Men; **39**—of Custom & Education; **43**—of Beauty; **50**—of Studies; **53**—of Praise; **56**—of Judicature; & **58**—of Vicissitude of Things]

Bacon : See below—UTOPIAS.

Baigent, Leigh, & Lincoln: Michael Baigent, Richard Leigh, & Henry Lincoln *The Messianic Legacy* 1986

Bakalar : See below—Grinspoon & Bakalar.

Barker : Ernest Barker *The Political Thought of Plato and Aristotle* 1918 [1959]

Barrow : John D. Barrow *Theories of Everything: the quest for ultimate explanation* 1991

Baum : Frank L. Baum *The Wizard of Oz* [fiction] 1900 [1956]

Beard : Charles A. Beard [1874-1948] *An Economic Interpretation of the Constitution of the United States* 1913 [renewed © 1941] [1964]

Bello : Nino Lo Bello *The Vatican Empire: a report on papal wealth* 1968

3° **Berger & Luckman** : Peter L. Berger & Thomas Luckman *The Social Construction of Reality* 1966

Berlin : Isaiah Berlin *The Crooked Timber of Humanity* 1991

Bernards : Neal Bernards, editor *War on Drugs: opposing viewpoints series* [collection of articles]1990

Berry : Arthur Berry *A short History of Astronomy: from earliest times through the 19th century* 1898 [1961]

Best : J. B. Best *Upstairs at the White House* [chief Usher from 1941..1969] 1973

1° **Bettelheim** : Bruno Bettelheim *The Uses of Enchantment: the meaning and importance of fairy tales* 1976

Bezymenski : Lev Bezymenski *The Death of Hitler* [in regard to rumors of single testicle] 1968

Bickerton : Derek Bickerton *Language and Species* 1990

Bird : Caroline Bird *The Case Against College* 1975

Blahut : Richard E. Blahut *Theory and Practice of Error Control Codes* [a text—in regard to communication errors in general]1983

Blair : Clay Blair *The Forgotten War: America in Korea 1950-1953* [in regard to asynchronous history as it seeks to re-appraise battle and biography in general] 1987

Blassingame : John W. Blassingame, editor *Slave Testimony* [Collection of Testimonials]1977

Bloch & Reddaway : Sidney Bloch & Peter Reddaway *Psychiatric Terror: how soviet psychiatry is used to suppress dissent* 1977

Bok : Sissela Bok *Lying: moral choice in public and private life* 1978 [1989]

Bouvior : Simone De Bouvior *The Second Sex* 1960

Braithwaite : R. B. Braithwaite *Scientific Explanation: a study of the function of theory, probability and law in science* 1946 [1955]

Brecher : Edward M. Brecher, editor *The Consumer's Union Report Licit and illicit Drugs* [1972]

Brown : William Hill Brown [1765-1793] *Power of Symphony* [fiction] 1789

Brunner : John Brunner *Stand on Zanzibar* [fiction] 1968

Buckley : Kevin Buckley *Panama: the whole story* [American efforts to capture/kidnap Noriega] 1991

Bugliosi : Vincent T. Bugliosi *Drugs in America: the case for victory* 1991

Bumcrot : See above—Althoen & Bumcrot

Bunyon : John Bunyon [1628-1688] *The Pilgrim's Progress* [fiction] 1678

Burgess : Anthony Burgess *A Clockwork Orange* [fiction] 1962 [1963]

Burton-Roberts : Noel Burton-Roberts *Analyzing Sentences: an introduction to English syntax* 1986 [1990]

Bury : J. B. Bury [1861-1927] *The Idea of Progress: an inquiry into its origin and growth* 1932 [1987]

Butcher : See above—Aristotle.

Byron : George Gordon Byron [1788-1824] *Don Juan* [satiric poem] 1819-1824

• C

Calvin : John Calvin [1509-1564] *Institutes of the Christian Religion* 1536

Camp : See below—de Camp.

Campbell : Joseph Campbell [1904-1987] *Primitive Myth: the masks of god* 1959 [1976]

Campbell : Joseph Campbell [1904-1987] *Creative Myth: the masks of god* 1968 [1971]

Campbell & Robinson : Joseph Campbell, & Henry Morton Robinson *A Skeleton's Key to Finnegan's Wake* 1944

Cantor : Norman F. Cantor *The Civilization of the middle Ages: medieval history, the life and death of a civilization* 1963 [1993]

Cantor : Norman F. Cantor *Inventing the Middle Ages: the lives, works, and ideas of the great medievalists of the 20th century* 1991

Cantor: Cantor & Werthman : ed, Norman F. Cantor, Michael S. Werthman *The History of Popular Culture* 1968

Caplow & McGee : Theodore Caplow, & Reece J. McGee *The Academic Marketplace: an anatomy of the academic profession...its mores, its morale, its machinations* 1958 [1965]

Capps : Alton C. Capps, editor *The Bible as Literature* 1971

Capra: Fritjof Capra *The Tao of Physics 197x* [Compare with Gary Zukav *The Dancing Wu Li Masters* 1979]

Carey : John Carey, editor *Eyewitness to History* [collection of articles] 1987

Carlson : Rick Carlson *The End of Medicine* 1975

Cash : W. J. Cash *The Mind of the South* 1941 [1991]

Castanda : Carlos Castanda *The Teachings of Don Juan: a Yaqui way of knowledge* [autobiographical fiction] 1968 [A cult classic. Carlos started out in this book as an anthropological student bent on examining the use of hallucinogens via the Yaqui mage—Don Juan. He ended up by book three, four, five, six, etc of this never ending gonzo journal to keep his lifestyle alive. Still, it is a 'classic' if for no other reason than it defies finding a genre, much less a 'different way of knowledge'. Suspiciously, Don Juan seems to borrow from a variety of basic religious aphorisms without any formal training other than say, a young anthropological student might find during the course of securing his degree]

Chan & Faruqi & Kitagawa & Raju : Wing-Tsit Chan, Isma'il Ragi al Faruqi, Joseph M. Kitagawa, P. T. Raju *The great Asian Religions: an anthology* 1969

Chardin : Teilhard de Chardin [1699-1779] *The Phenomenon of Man* 1955 [1975]

Charles : C. M. Charles *Elementary Classroom Management* 1983

Chernow : Ron Chernow *The House of Morgan: an American banking dynasty and the rise of modern finance* 1990

2° **Church** : Robert L. Church *Education in the United States: an interpretive History* 1976

3° **Cialdini** : Robert B. Cialdini *Influence: how and why people agree to things* 1984

Clausewitz : Carl von Clausewitz [1780-1831] *Vom Kriege* [translation— *On War*] [written from 1818 until 1830; he died the next year]

Clough & Cole : Shepard Bancroft Clough, & Charles Woolsey Cole *Economic History of Europe* 1952 [1966]

Cole, Charles : See previous—Clough & Cole.

Cole, Lewis : See below—Hiliard & Cole.

Collingwood : R. G. Collingwood *The Idea of History* 1946 [Oxford revised edition—1994]

Comte : Auguste Comte [1798-1857] *Positive Philosophy* [original—*Cours de philosophie positive* 6 volumes] 1829-1842

Coser : ed, Lewis A. Coser *The Pleasures of Sociology* [collection of 36 essays] 1980

Consumer : *The Consumer's Union Report Licit and Illicit Drugs* [1972]

Crosland : M. P. Crosland Historical *Studies in the Language of Chemistry* 1962 [1978] [in regard to metaphorical treatments in general]

Cuppy : Will Cuppy *The Decline and Fall of Practically Everybody* [short biographies] 1950

• D

3° **d'Abro** : A. d'Abro *The Evolution of Scientific Thought: from Newton to Einstein* 1927

Dannen : Fredric Dannen *Hit Men* [in regard to the politics of culture in general, & the record industry in specific] 1990

Darwin : Charles (Robert) Darwin [1809-1882] *On the Origin of Species* ...1859

Darwin : Charles (Robert) Darwin [1809-1882] *Descent of Man* 1871

David-Neel : Alexandra David-Neel *Magic & Mystery in Tibet* 1929 [1971]

2° **Davis & Hersh** : Philip J. Davis, & Reuben Hersh *The Mathematical Experience* [in regard to math illiteracy] 1981

2° **de Camp** : L. Sprague de Camp *The Ancient Engineers* 19xx

DeCell : See below—Lichtman & DeCell.

de Chardin : See above—Chardin.

Defoe : Daniel Defoe [1660-1731] *The shortest Way with Dissenters* [pamphlet] 1702

Defoe : Daniel Defoe [1660-1731] *Moll Flanders* [fiction] 1722

Defoe : Daniel Defoe [1660-1731] *Robinson Crusoe* [fiction] 1719

de Molina : See below—Molina.

de Montaigne : See below—Montaigne.

de Sade : See below—Sade.

Denise : See above—Albert & Denise & Peterfreund.

Denton : Jeremiah A. Denton, JR. *When Hell was in Session* [war autobiography] 1982?

DeRopp : Robert S. DeRopp *Drugs & the Mind* 1958

Descartes : René Descartes [1596-1650] *Rules for the Direction of the Mind* [self notes] 1701

Detmold : M(ichael) J. Detmold *The Unity of Law and Morality: a refutation of legal positivism* 1984 de Tocqueville : See below—Tocqueville.

2° **Dewey** : John Dewey [1859-1952] *Dewey on Education: selections* 1959

2° **Dewey** : John Dewey [1859-1952] *Philosophy of Education* [1935-1945] 1956

Dickens : Charles (John Huffam) Dickens [1812-1870] *A Christmas Carol* [fiction] 1843

DiIulio : John J. DiIulio, JR. *No Escape: the future of American corrections* 1991

Don Juan : fictitious character regarded as a symbol of—the Libertine. Originated in popular legend, his first literary appearance was in the tragic drama *El Burlador de Sevilla* 1630 [translated as *The Love Rogue*] by Spanish dramatist Tirso de Molina. He likewise appears in Mozart's opera *Don Giovanni* 1787.

Don Juan is admired for his vitality, his arrogant courage, and his sense of humor. He is lead to his destruction by the flippant course of his life which gathers a crowd of enemies. He is comparable in many respects with the characters—Don Quixote, Hamlet, and Faust. Don Juan is reborn, but not very well in T. Shadwell's *The Libertine* 1676. In Byron's satiric poem *Don Juan* 1819-1824. And in George Bernard Shaw's drama *Man and Superman* 1903.

Indeed, there are many incarnations for capricious love.

Donzelot : J. Donzelot *The Policing of Families: welfare versus the state* 1980

1° **Doren** : Charles Van Doren *The Idea of Progress* 1967

Dougherty & Hammack : Kevin J. Dougherty, & Floyd M. Hammack, editors *Education and Society: a reader* [collection of articles] 1990

Douglass : Frederick (Augustus Washington Bailey) Douglass [1817-1895] *Life and Times of Frederick Douglass* 1892

2° **Drake** : William Earle Drake *Intellectual Foundations of Modern Education* 1967

Dubos : René Dubos *The Mirage of Health: utopian progress and biological change* 1959

• E

Ebenstien & Pritchett & Turner : William Ebenstien, C. Herman Pritchett, Henry A. Turner, Dean Mann *American Democracy in world Perspective* [a text—in regard to education as social control] 1967

Eddy : Daniel Eddy *Young Man's Friend* 1857?

Einstein : Albert Einstein. See below. firsthand accounts in—Shamos.

Eliot : T(homas) S(tearns) Eliot [1888-1965] *The Hollow Men* [poem] 1925

Ellul : Jacque Ellul *The Technological System* 1980

2° **Ellul** : Jacque Ellul *Propaganda: the formation of men's attitudes* 1965

1° **Ellul** : Jacque Ellul *The Political Illusion* 1967

1° **Ellul** : Jacque Ellul *The Technological Society* 1964

Ellul : Jacque Ellul *Violence: reflections from a Christian perspective* 1969

Ellul : Jacques Ellul *The Politics of GOD, the Politics of Man* 1972 [1977]

Engels : See below—Marx & Engels.

Engerman : See below—Fogal & Engerman.

Erikson : Erik H. Erikson *Childhood and Society* [second edition] 1950 [1963]

• F

Faruqi : See above—Chan & Faruqi & Kitagawa & Raju.

Faulkner : Harold Underwood Faulkner *American Economic History* [eighth edition] 1924 [1960]

Finch : Henry Le Roy Finch *Wittgenstein—the early philosophy: an exposition of the 'Tractatus'* 1971

1° **Fiedler** : Leslie Fiedler *Love and Death in American Literature* 1960 [1992]

Fiedler : Leslie Fiedler *The Return of the vanishing American* 1968

Fiedler : Leslie Fiedler *Waiting for the End* 1964

Fiedler : Leslie Fiedler *What is Literature?* 1984

Fielding : Henry Fielding [1707-1754] *An Apology for the Life of Mrs. Shamela Andrews* [fiction] [published 1741]

Fielding : Henry Fielding [1707-1754] *The History of Tom Jones, a Foundling* [fiction] 1749

Findlay : Bruce Allyn Findlay, & Ester Blair Findlay *Your Rugged Constitution* 1950 [1952]

Fletcher : Joseph Fletcher *Situation Ethics: the new morality* 1966

3° **Fogal & Engerman** : Robert W. Fogal, & Stan L. Engerman *Time on the Cross* 1974 [two volumes. NOTE: second volume is mostly an explanation of their statistical methodology and sources]

Foucault : M. Foucault *Madness and Civilization* 1971

Frank & Rosenthal : Mel Frank & Ed Rosenthal *Marijuana Grower's Guide* 1978

Franklin : Benjamin Franklin [1706-1790] *From Observations Concerning the Increase of Mankind* 1751

Frazer : J(ames) (George) Frazer [1854-1941] *The Golden Bough: a study in magic and religion* [9 volumes]

Frazier : J. Frazier *The Marijuana Farmers, Hemp Cults, and Cultures* 1974

Freud : Sigmund Freud [1856-1939] *The Interpretation of Dreams* 1899

Freud : Sigmund Freud [1856-1939] *Jokes and their Relation to the Unconscious* 1905

Freud : Sigmund Freud [1856-1939] *Civilization and its Discontents* 1958

Freud : See ALSO—Philip Rieff. [an edited collection of Freud's papers concerning therapy & therapeutic techniques]

Friedan : Betty Friedan *The Feminine Mystique* 1963

Friedman : Richard Elliott Friedman *Who Wrote the Bible?* 1987

Froebel : Friedrich (Wilhelm August) Froebel [1782-1852] *A Family Book for developing the self Activity of Children* 1845

Froebel : Friedrich (Wilhelm August) Froebel [1782-1852] *The Education of Man* 1826

Fukuyama : Francis Fukuyama *The End of History and the Last Man* 1992

• G

Galileo : Galilei Galileo [1564-1642] *Dialogue concerning Two New Sciences...*1638 [1914]

Galileo : Galilei Galileo [1564-1642] *Dialogue concerning the two chief world Systems—Ptolemaic and Copernican* 1632 [1953]

Galileo : Galilei Galileo. See below. firsthand accounts in—Shamos.

2° **Gardner** : John Gardner *The Art of Fiction: notes on the craft for young writers* 1983

Geertz : Clifford Geertz *The Interpretation of Cultures* [collection of essays] 1973 [in specific, 4ß-5A/14a—the conceptual morass of defining culture; 16b/25a/26b—cultural analysis; 18A—coherence; 22ß—natural laboratory; And the two quotes found pg 27 fn 5, and pg 29b]

Gerstein & Green : Dean R. Gerstein, & Lawrence W. Green, editors *Preventing Drug Abuse: what do we know?* 1993

Gillispie : Charles Coulston Gillispie *The Edge of Objectivity: an Essay in the History of Scientific Ideas* 1960.

Glenn & Robinson : Jerome Clayton Glenn, & George S. Robinson *Space Trek: the endless migration* 1978

Goddard : H. H. Goddard *Feeble-Mindedness: its causes and consequences* 1914

1° **Godement** : Godement *Algebra* [Houghton Mifflin Publishers] [Fundamentals of Axiomatics—that is, abstract Algebra] [translated from the French—*Algebra*] 19xx

Goebbels : (Paul) Joseph Goebbels [1897-1945] *Wesen und Gestalt des National Soczialismus* [literal translation Essence and Form in National Socialism] [in regard to effective use of propaganda] 1935

Goebbels : (Paul) Joseph Goebbels. See ALSO—ed, Louis P. Lochner *The Goebbels Diaries* 1948

Goethe : Johann Wolfgang von Goethe [1749-1832] *The Sorrows of Young Werther* [fiction] 1774

Golding : William Golding [1911-?] *The Lord of the Flies* [fiction] 1954

Goodman : Paul Goodman *Growing Up Absurd* 1956 [1960]

Goodman : Paul Goodman *Utopian Essays and practical Proposals* [collection of articles] 1962 [See more specifically the chapters labeled— Utopian Thinking; Post-Christian Man; & My Psychology as a 'Utopian Sociologist']

Gould : Stephan Jay Gould *Ever Since Darwin: reflections in natural history* 1973 [1977]

Gould : Stephan Jay Gould *The Panda's Thumb* 1980

2° **Gould** : Stephan Jay Gould *The Mismeasure of Man* 1981

Gould : Stephan Jay Gould *Hen's Teeth and Horse's Toes* 1983 [1984]

Gould & Truitt : ed, James A. Gould, Willis H. Truitt *Political Ideologies* [collection of essays] 1973

Graham : A(ngus) C(harles) Graham *Disputers of the Tao: philosophical argument in ancient China* 1989 [1993] Illinois : Open Court Publishing Co

3° **Graves** : Robert (Ranke) Graves [1895-1985] *The White Goddess* 1978

Green : See above—Gerstein & Green.

Grinspoon : Lester Grinspoon *Marihuana Reconsidered* [second edition] 1971 [1994]

Grinspoon & Bakalar : Lester Grinspoon, & James B. Bakalar *Cocaine: a drug and its social evolution* 1976

• H

Haines : Helen E. Haines *Living with Books* [in regard to library science] 1935

Hamilton & Jay & Madison : Hamilton, Jay, Madison *The Federalist* [1787-88]

Hammack : See above—Dougherty & Hammack.

Hamowy : ed, Ronald Hamowy *Dealing with Drugs: consequences of government control* [collection of articles] 1987 [1990]

Handy : Charles Handy *The Age of Unreason* 1989

Harrington : Michael Harrington *The Other Americans* 1962

Heidegger : Martin Heidegger [1889-1976] *Kant and the Problem of Metaphysics* 1931

Heilbroner & Thurow : Robert Heilbroner, & Lester Thurow *Economics Explained* 1982

Heilbroner : Robert L. Heilbroner *The Worldly Philosophers: the lives, times, and ideas of the great economic thinkers* 1953

Heppenheimer : T. A. Heppenheimer *Colonies in Space* 1978

Herbart : Johann Friedrich Herbart [1776-1841] *A Textbook in Psychology* 1894

Herbart : Johann Friedrich Herbart [1776-1841] *Outline of Pedagogical Lectures* 1835

Herbart : Johann Friedrich Herbart [1776-1841] *Outlines of Education Doctrine* 1901

Herbart : Johann Friedrich Herbart [1776-1841] *The Science of Education* 1806

Herder : Johann Gottfried von Herder [1744-1803] *Von deutshcher Art und Kunst* [translation—*Of German Art and Artifice*]

Hersh : See above—Davis & Hersh.

Heyman : Tom Heyman *On an Average Day* [popular reference concerning U.S. statistics] 1989

Hietala : Thomas R. Hietala *Manifest Design: anxious aggrandizement in late Jackson's America* 1985

Hiliard & Cole : David Hiliard, & Lewis Cole *This Side of Glory: the auto-biography of David Hilliard and the story of the black panther party* [autobiographical fiction] 1993

Hirsch : E. D. Hirsch, JR. *Cultural Literacy: what every American needs to know* 199x

Hitler : Adolf Hitler [1889-1945] *Mein Kampf* 1925

Hobbes : Thomas Hobbes [1588-1679] *Leviathan: or the form and power of a commonwealth ecclesiastical and civil* 1651

Hogan: Daniel B. Hogan *The Regulation of psychotherapists* 1979

volume 1—*A Study in Philosophy & Practice of professional Regulation*

volume 2—*A handbook of State Licensure Laws*

volume 3—*A Review of malpractice Suits in the United States*

volume 4—*A Resource Bibliography*

Horne : See below—Van Horne.

Hoving : Thomas Hoving *Making the Mummies Dance: inside the metro-politan museum of art* 1993 [an exemplum of political workings in the business of art]

Hoyt : Robert S. Hoyt *Europe in the middle Ages* 2nd Edition 1957 [1966]

Hunt & Sherman : E. K. Hunt, and Howard J. Sherman *Economics: an introduction to traditional and radical views* 1981

Huxley : Aldous Leonard Huxley [1894-1963] *Brave New World* [fiction] 1932

Huxley : Aldous Leonard Huxley [1894-1963] *The Perennial Philosophy* 1944 [1962]

Huxley : Aldous Leonard Huxley [1894-1963] *The Doors of Perception* [self-Reflections] 1954

Huxley, Julius : See below—Notestein.

Huxley : T(homas) H(enry) Huxley *Science & Culture* 1881 [i.e. this is Aldous' grandfather]

Huxley : T(homas) H(enry) Huxley *Evolution & Ethics* 1893

• I

3° Illich : Ivan Illich *DeSchooling Society* 1971

Illich : Ivan Illich *Medical Nemesis* 1976

Illich : Ivan Illich *Gender* 1982

Ingleby : D. Ingleby *Critical Psychiatry: the politics of mental health* 1981

Irving : Washington Irving [1783-1859] *The Sketch Book of Geoffrey Crayon, Gentleman* [fiction] [1819-1820]

Iyer : Raghavan Iyer *Parapolitics: toward the city of man* 1979

1° Izard : Carroll E. Izard *Human Emotions* [text] 1977

• J

Jackson : See below—Linskens & Jackson.

Jacobs : Jane Jacobs *The Death and Life of great American Cities* 1961

Jaffe : Bernard Jaffe *Crucibles: the story of chemistry from ancient alchemy to nuclear fission* 1930 [1976]

James : William James [1842-1910] *The Principles of Psychology* 2 volumes 1890 [1950]

James : William James [1842-1910] *The Varieties of Religious Experience* 1902 [1936]

James : William James [1842-1910] *The Sentiment of Rationality* 1905

Jay : See above—Hamilton & Jay & Madison.

1° **Jaynes** : Julian Jaynes *The Origin of Consciousness in the Breakdown of the Bicameral Mind* 1976

Jones : Jeremiah Jones *The lost Books of the Bible* 1926 [1979]

Josephy : Alvin M. Josephy, JR. *On the Hill: a history of the American congress from 1789 to present* (MORE at 1789 to 1979) 1979

Joyce : James Joyce [1882-1941] *Finnegans Wake* [fiction] 1939

Judson : Horace Freeland Judson *The Eighth Day of Creation: the makers of the revolution in biology* 1979 [an exemplum of the misapplication of the concepts of science, vs. engineering, vs. technology] See ALSO—Rhodes.

Jung : Carl Jung *The Undiscovered Self* 1957 [1958]

Jung : ed, Carl Jung *Man and his Symbols* [collection of articles by Carl Jung, M.-L. von Franz, Joseph L. Henderson, Lolande Jacobi, Aniela Jaffé] 1968 [1969]

• K

Kahler : Erich Kahler *Man the Measure: a new approach to history* 1943 [1961] [A post WWII attempt to re-evaluate man, though unstated, in light of a philosophy of history]

Kamin : See below—Lewontin & Rose & Kamin.

Kant : Immanuel Kant [1724-1804] *The one possible Basis for a Demonstration of the Existence of GOD* [essay] 1762

1° **Kant** : Immanuel Kant [1724-1804] *The Critique of Pure Reason* 1787

Kant : Immanuel Kant [1724-1804] *Religion within the Limits of Reason Alone* 1793

Karnow : Stanley Karnow *Vietnam: a History* 1983

Kazamias : See below—Nash & Kazamias & Perkinson.

Keegan : John Keegan *A History of Warfare* 1993

Keesing : Felix M. Keesing *Cultural Anthropology: the science of custom* 1958

Kerr : John Kerr *A Most Dangerous Method: the story of Jung, Freud, and Sabina Spielrein* [biography] 1993

Keynes : John Maynard Keynes [1883-1946] *The General Theory of Employment, Interest, and Money* [collated in 1935 and published in 1936]

Khalil : Samir al-Khalil *Republic of Fear: inside Story of Saddam's Iraq* 1989

Kindleberger : Charles P. Kindleberger *Manias, Panics, and Crashes* 1989

Kitagawa : See above—Chan & Faruqi & Kitagawa & Raju.

Kitcher : Philip Kitcher Vaulting *Ambition: sociobiology and the quest for human nature* 1985 [1990]

Knudtson : See below—Suzuki & Knudtson.

Koch & Peden : editors, A. Koch and W. Peden *The Life and Selected Writings of Thomas Jefferson* 1944

Koch : G. A. Koch *Republican Religion* 1933

Kostelanetz : Richard Kostelanetz *The End of intelligent Writing: literary politics in America* 1973 [1974]

Kubie : L. S. Kubie *Psychiatric and psychoanalytic Considerations of the Problems of Consciousness* in ed, E. Adrean et AL *Brain Mechanisms and Consciousness* 1954

2° **Kübler-Ross** : Elisabeth Kübler-Ross *Death: the final stage of growth* 1975

Kuhn : Thomas S. Kuhn [1922-?] *The Structure of Scientific Revolutions* 2nd ed. 1962 [1970]

• L

LaFeber : Walter LaFeber *Inevitable Revolutions: the united states in central America* 1983

LaFeber : Walter LaFeber *The American Age: u.s. foreign policy at home and abroad since* 1750 1989

Lakatos & Musgrave : editors, Imre Lakatos, & Alan Musgrave *Criticism and the Growth of Knowledge* 1970 [1977]

Lawrence : D(avid) H(erbert) Lawrence [1885-1930] *Studies in classic American Literature*

Lawrence : D(avid) H(erbert) Lawrence [1885-1930] *The Symbolic Meaning* 1923 [1964]

Leigh : Richard Leigh. See above—Baigent, Leigh & Lincoln.

Leven : Jeremy Leven *Satan, his Therapy and Cure by the unfortunate Dr. Kassler J.S.P.S.* [fiction] 1982

Lewis : Clarence Irving Lewis *Mind and the world Order: outline of a theory of knowledge* 1929 [1956]

2° **Lewis** : C(live) S(taples) Lewis [1898-1963] *Mere Christianity* 1943 [1952]

Lewontin & Rose & Kamin : R. C. Lewontin, Steven Rose, & Leon J. Kamin *NOT in our Genes: biology, ideology, and human nature* 1984

Lichtman & DeCell : Allan J. Lichtman & Ken DeCell *The Keys to the Presidency: prediction without Polls* [subtitle continues—the revolutionary system that reveals how presidential elections really work from the civil war to the 21st century. Lanham, Maryland: Madison Books] 1970

Lifton : Robert Jay Lifton *The Broken Connection* 1979

Lifton : Robert Jay Lifton *The Nazi Doctors* 1986

Lincoln : Henry Lincoln. See above—Baigent, Leigh & Lincoln.

Linskens & Jackson : editors, H. F. Linskens, & J. F. Jackson *Wine Analysis* [in regard to complex research similarities between the plants *Cannabis* & *Vitis vinifera* leading to their own classic end products] 1988

Lo Bello : See above—Bello.

Lochner : ed, Louis P. Lochner *The Goebbels Diaries* 1948

Locke : John Locke [1632-1704] *The Second Treatise of Government* 1690 [in specific, chapter ix: *of the Ends of political Society & Government*, and chapter xix—*of the dissolution of Government*]

Locke : John Locke [1632-1704] *Essay concerning Human Understanding* 1690 [tedious reading, but in general to be read from the perspective of education]

Lombroso : Cesare Lombroso [1836-1909] *L'uomo delinquente* [translation *The Criminal Man*] 1876

Lowel Offering : See below—Periodical.

Luckman : See above—Berger & Luckman.

Lucretius : Titus Lucretius Carus [circa 96-55 B.C.] *De Rerum Natura* [translation by Charles E. Bennett *On the Nature of Things* 1946] [an invocation to the allusions of the world, i.e. Substance is eternal, Void exists, 'atoms' are indivisible, etc]

Lyell : Charles Lyell *Principles of Geology* [first volume] 1830 [second volume—1831; third volume—1833. Note that Charles' book is mostly of facts, & not of principles. It is this novel method of teaching via facts that is, in effect, the principle. A practice considered in his day as heretical to the notion of 'scientific inquiry'. ALSO NOTE—most of the 'revolutionary' material attributed to Charles Darwin; Darwin, in fact, learned from Charles Lyell.]

• M

Machiavelli : Niccoló Machiavelli [1469-1527] *Il Principe* 1513 [translated by Luigi Ricci, revised by E. R. P. Vincent *The Prince*]

Madison : See above—Hamilton & Jay & Madison.

Maimonides : Moses Maimonides *The Guide for the Perplexed* 1135-1168 [first English version 1904]

Maine : Henry Sumner Maine [1822-1888] *Ancient Law* 1864

Malthus, Thomas : See below—Notestein.

Manheim : Leonard & Eleanor Manheim *Hidden Patterns: studies in psychoanalytic literary criticism* 1966 [1968]

Marivaux : Pierre (Carlet de Champlain de) Marivaux [1688-1763] *La Vie de Marianne* [translation—*The Life of Marianne*] [fiction] 1731-41

Martin : Judith Martin *Common Courtesy: in which Miss Manners solves the problem that baffled Mr. Jefferson* 1985

Marty : Martin E. Marty *Religion and Republic: the American circumstance* 1987

Marx & Engels : Karl Marx, & Friedrich Engels *The Communist Manifesto* 1848

Mather : Cotton Mather [1663-1728] *Magnolia Christi American* 1702

Mather : ed, Richard Mather [1596-1669] *Bay Psalm Book* 1640

Matthiessen : F. O. Matthiessen *American Renaissance* 1941

McGee : See above—Caplow & McGee.

McKeown & McLachlan : Thomas McKeown, Gordon McLachlan *Medical History and Medical Care: a symposium of perspectives* 1971

McLachlan : See Above—McKeown & McLachlan.

McNeill : William H. McNeill *Plagues and Peoples* 1976 [in regard to disease pandemics & their historical effects. Compare with the plague & A.I.D.s]

Meeks : Wayne A. Meeks *The Origins of Christian Morality: the first two centuries* 1993

Merrill & Sedgwick : Robert E. Merrill, & Henry D. Sedgwick *The New Venture Handbook* 1987 [startup ventures for small business men— in regard to big business methods applied to small]

Meyer : Adolphe E. Meyer *An Educational History of the western World* 1965

Miller : William Lee Miller *The First Liberty: religion and the American republic* 1985

Misner & Thorne & Wheeler : Charles W. Misner, Kip S. Thorne, & John Archibald Wheeler *Gravitation* [in regard to circularity of definitions, complexity of mathematics, lack of clarity in thought, and disguised metaphors in general; in relation to Einstein's concept of relativity in specific] 1970 [1973]

Molina : Tirso de Molina (pseudonym of Gabriel Tellez) [1584-1648] *El Burlador de Sevilla* [translated as—*The Love Rogue*] [fiction] 1630

Monmouth : Geoffry of Monmouth [1100-1154/1155] *Historia Regum Britannicae* [translation—*History of the Kings of Britain*]

Monsen & Walters : R. Joseph Monsen, & Kenneth D. Walters *Nationalized Companies: a threat to American business* 1983

Montaigne : Michel Eyquem de Montaigne [1533-1592] *Essays* 1580 [1981]

Monte : Christopher F. Monte *Beneath the Mask: an introduction to theories of personality* [a sampling of classic psychological theories concerning human nature'. What makes this book of interest is that the odd personality traits of the theorists themselves is likewise explored—Freud, Erikson, Jung, Adler, Sullivan, Laing, Kelly, Horney, Fromm, Aliport, Maslow, Rogers, Skinner, Bandura, & Eysenck] 1977 [1987]

More : Thomas More *Utopia* [fiction. See also—UTOPIAS] 1518

Morgan : H. Wayne Morgan *Americas Road to Empire: the war with Spain and overseas expansion* 1965

Morris, Henry : See below—Whitcomb & Morris.

Morris : Herbert M. Morris *Deism in 18th Century America* 1934

Mozart : Wolfgang Amadeus Mozart [1756-1791] *Don Giovanni* [an opera] 1787

Murrow : Edward R. Murrow *'Harvest of Shame'* [T.V. Documentary]

Musgrave : See above—Lakatos & Musgrave.

Mun : Thomas Mun [1571-1641] *England's Treasure by Forraign Trade* (sic) [discourse] 1664

• N

Nash & Kazamias & Perkinson : Paul Nash, Andreas M. Kazamias, & Henry J. Perkinson *The Educated Man: studies in the history of educational thought* 1965

Neel : See above—David-Neel.

Newton : Issac Newton [1642-1727] *Philosopiae Naturalis Principia Mathematica* [circa 1789]

Newton : Issac Newton See below. firsthand Accounts in—Shamos.

Nichols : John Nichols *The Nirvana Blues* [fiction] 1981

Niebuhr : H. Richard Niebuhr *Christ & Culture* 1951

Nietzsche : Friedrich Nietzsche [1844-1900] *Thus spake Zarathustra* 1883-85 [1961]

Nietzsche : Friedrich Nietzsche [1844-1900] *The Will to Power* 1901/1910-11 in *Basic Writings of Nietzsche* 1968 [NOTE: the date discrepancy is due to the publication of these unpolished notes by Nietzsche's sister following upon his death]

Noss : John B. Noss *Man's Religions* [a text—general reference] 1974

Notestein : Frank W. Notestein, editor? *Three Essays on Population— Thomas Malthus, Julian Huxley, & Frederick Osborn* 1956 Mentor Books [1960]

3° **Novak** : Michael Novak *The Spirit of Democratic Capitalism* 1982

• O

O'Neill : Gerard K. O'Neill *The High Frontier* 1976? [in regard to the colonization of space, scientific hope, technical expectations]

O'Neill & Swisher : ed, Terry O'Neill, & Karin L. Swisher *Economics in America: opposing viewpoints* 1992

O'Rourke : P. J. O'Rourke *Give War a Chance* [gonzo journalism] 1992

O'Rourke: P. J. O'Rourke *Parliament of Whores* [gonzo journalism] 1991

Osborn, Frederick : See above—Notestein.

Otis : Arthur S. Otis *Light Velocity and Relativity: the problem of light velocity. Einstein theory found invalid, a classical theory of relativity, a challenge to young scientists* 3rd ed. 1963

• P

Pacioli : Lucas Pacioli *Summa de Arithmetica, Geometria, Proportioni and Proportionalita* 1494

Paine : Thomas Paine *The Age of Reason: a treatise on the nature of religion and state* 1948

Park : Joe Park, editor *Selected Readings in the Philosophy of Education* [collection of articles] 1968

Paulos : John Allen Paulos *Innumeracy: math illiteracy and its consequences* 1988

Peck : M. Scott Peck *The Road Less Travelled* 1978 [The bible of the new therapeutic religions. Compare—Marianne Williamson's *A Return to Love*]

Peden : See above—Koch & Peden.

PERIODICAL: *'The Lowel Offering'* [1840-1845]

PERIODICAL : See ALSO—Betty Arras *'California Monitor of Education'*

Perkinson : See above—Nash & Kazamias & Perkinson.

Peterfreund : See above—Albert & Denise & Peterfreund.

Phillips & Wynne : Joël L. Phillips, & Ronald D. Wynne *Cocaine: the mystique and the reality* 1980

Plato : Plato *Republic* [Plato's lifespan 428-348/347 B.C.E.]

Poe : Edgar Allen Poe—See Stern *The Portable Poe*

Polya : G. Polya *Mathematics and Plausible Reasoning* volume 1: *induction and analogy in mathematics* 1954 [1990]

Popper : Karl R. Popper [1902-?] *The Logic of Scientific Discovery* 1959 [1st German 1934]

Popper : Karl R. Popper *The Open Society and its Enemies: 1962* [1971] volume 1: *the spell of Plato* volume 2: *the high tide of prophecy—Hegel and Marx*

Prévost : Eugene-Marcel Prévost *Les Demi-Vierges* [translation—*The Half Virgins*] [fiction] 1894

Price : Derek J. de Solla Price *Little Science, Big Science* 1963

Pritchett : See above—Ebenstien & Pritchett & Turner.

Proger : Samuel Proger, editor *The Medicated Society* 1968 [the ritualization of drug-taking and the creation of its subculture. That is, prescription, not casual drugs.]

• R

Raju : See above—Chan & Faruqi & Kitagawa & Raju.

Rayback : Joseph G. Rayback *A History of American Labor* 1959 [1966]

Rea : Mary-Alice F. Rea *'Early Introduction of Economic Plants into New England'* [article in the periodical] Econ. Botany 29 (4): pp 333-356

Reddaway : See above—Bloch & Reddaway.

Reps : Paul Reps *Zen Bones, Zen Flesh: a collection of zen and pre-zen writings* Anchor Books [No publication date] circa 1934/1935/1939

Rhodes : Richard Rhodes *The Making of the Atomic Bomb* 1986 [a typical exemplum of the misapplication of the concepts of science vs. engineering vs. technology] See ALSO—Judson.

Rice : Edward Rice *Captain Sir Richard Francis Burton* [biography] 1900

2° **Richards** : I(vor) A(rmstrong) Richards [1893-¿] *Practical Criticism: a study of literary judgment* 1929 [The entire book is of interest, but for this study especially chapter one; & pp 174-181]

Richards : Janet Radcliffe Richards *The skeptical Feminist: a philosophical enquiry* 1980

Richards : Leonard L. Richards *Gentlemen of property and standing: anti-Abolition Mobs in Jackson's America* 1970

Richardson : Samuel Richardson [1689-1761] *Clarissa—the History of a young Lady* [fiction] 1747- 48

Richardson : Samuel Richardson [1689-1761] *Pamela, or virtue rewarded* [fiction] 1740

Ridgeway : James Ridgeway *The Closed Corporation: American universities in crisis* 1968

Rieff : ed, Philip Rieff Freud—*Therapy & Technique: essays on dream inter-pretation, hypnosis, transference, free association, and other techniques of psychoanalysis* 1963

Rius : Rius *Marx for Beginners* 1976

Robinson, George S. : See above—Glenn & Robinson.

Robinson, Henry Morton : See above—Campbell & Robinson.

Robinson : Harriet Hanson Robinson *Loom and Spindle* 1898

Robinson : John J. Robinson *Dungeon, Fire and Sword: the knights templar* 1991 [in regard to the ties between finance & faith]

Rodgers : Marion Elizabeth Rodgers, editor *The impossible H. L. Menken* [collection of news articles] 1991

Rose : See above—Lewontin & Rose & Kamin.

Rosenthal : See above—Frank & Rosenthal.

Ross : See above—Kübler-Ross.

Ross : Ralph Ross *Symbols & Civilization: science, morals, religion, art* 1957 [1962]

Ross : Shelly Ross *Fall from Grace: sex, scandal and corruption in American politics from 1702 to present* 1988

Rossabi : Morris Rossabi *Khubilai Khan: his life and times* [biography] 1988 [in regard to the reality of random violence of the past exceed-ing that of the abstract perception of violence in our present]

Roszak : Theodore Roszak *The Making of a Counter culture: reflections on the technocratic society and its youthful opposition* 1969 [in specific, chapter V: the counterfeit Infinity: the use and abuse of psychedelic experience; chap VI: exploring Utopia: the visionary sociology of Paul Goodman; & chap VII: the myth of objective consciousness]

Rothman : David J. Rothman *The Discovery of the Asylum: social order and disorder in the new republic* 1971 [1990]

Ruben : Joan Shelley Rubin *The Making of Middle Brow Culture* 1992 [In particular, chap 1: self, culture, and self-culture in America; chap 3: ...the early history of the Book of the Month Club; chap 5: ...Will Durant and the vogue of the 'outline']

Russell : Bertrand Russell [1872-1970] *Mysticism and Logic* 1917 [1957]

Russel & Whitehead : Bertrand Russel, & Alfred North Whitehead *Principia Mathematica* [1910 1913]

3° **Rychlak** : Joseph F. Rychlak *Introduction to Personality and Psychotherapy: a theory—construction approach* [a survey of major schools of personality theory & psychotherapy] 1973

• S

Sabbagh : Karl Sabbagh *Skyscraper* [an economic web of activities in exemplum] 1989

Sade : Marquis de Sade [Comte Donatien-Alphonse-François] *Juliette* 1797 [6 volumes in one—1968] [as one reviewer for the Library Journal noted, 'an amazing sequence of imaginatively bizarre sexual adventures punctuated by philosophical and theological digression.' Still outlawed in France.]

Saint Augustine : See above—Augustine.

Samhaber : Ernst Samhaber *Merchants Make History* 1960 [1964]

Sartre : Jean-Paul Sartre [1905-1980] *Being and Nothingness: a phenomenological essay on ontology* 1943

Savage : Marshall T. Savage *The Millennial Project: colonizing the galaxy in eight easy steps* 1992 [1994]

Schneider : Herbert W. Schneider *A History of American Philosophy* 1946 [1963]

Sedgwick : See above—Merrill & Sedgwick.

Selesnick : See—Alexander & Selesnick.

Seward : Jack Seward *Hara-Kiri: Japanese ritual suicide* 1968 [1973]

Shadwell : T(homas) Shadwell *The Libertine* [fiction] 1676

Shakir : M. H. Shakir, translator *The Qur'an* 1991 [in regard to mind censorship; and the Use of GOD as a political/economic End; & NOTE: the Qur'an (a.k.a. Koran) was never meant to be written, but only passed by word of mouth. The orthodox still consider its publication a sacrilege of the words of their prophet.]

Shamos : Morris H. Shamos, editor *Great Experiments in Physics: firsthand accounts from Galileo to Einstein* [Collection of first Treatises] 1959

Sharpe : Tom Sharpe *Riotous Assembly* [fiction] 19xx [you had better have a decent sense of what S. Africa under Apartheid is like before you begin. Because Mr. Sharpe's dark humor may leave some of you less than laughing. Still, it is an interesting caricature of how man, as member of a culture, can get caught up in the most superfluous of 'ideals'. This is a British Import, Pan Publishers, I believe]

Shaw : George Bernard Shaw [1856-1950] *Man and Superman* [drama] 1903

Shelly : Frank Shelly *Raiders and Rebels: the golden age of piracy* 1986 [in regard to economics]

Shelly : Mary Wollstonecraft Shelly [1797-1851] *Frankenstein or the modern Prometheus* [fiction] 1818

Shelly : Mary Wollstonecraft Shelly [1797-1851] *The Last Man* [fiction] 1826

Shelly : Mary Wollstonecraft Shelly [1797-1851] *Valperga: or, The Life and Adventures of Castruccio, Prince of Lucca* [fiction] 1823

Sherman : See above—Hunt & Sherman.

Silberman : Neil Asher Silberman *Digging for God and Country: exploration in the holy land* 1799-1917 1982

Skinner : B(urrhus) F(rederic) Skinner [1904-1990] *Beyond Freedom and Dignity* 1971

Skinner : B. F. Skinner [1904-1990] *Science and Human Behavior* 1953

Skinner : B. F. Skinner [1904-1990] *The Technology of Teaching* 1968

Skinner : B. F. Skinner [1904-1990] *Walden Two* [fiction] 1948 [1972]; see ALSO below—UTOPIAS.

Smith : Adam Smith [1723-1790] *An Inquiry into the Nature and Causes of the Wealth of Nations* 1776

Smith : David Smith *Reagan for Beginners* 1984

Snow : C(harles) P(ercy) Snow [1905-1980] *The Two Cultures* 1959

Solomon : Robert C. Solomon *About Love: reinventing romance for our time* 1988

Sophocles : Sophocles *Oedipus the King* [fiction] [Sophocles' lifespan 496-406 B.C.E]

Soule : George Soule *Ideas of the Great Economists* 1952

Spanier : John Spanier *Games Nations Play* 6th ed 1987

Spencer : Herbert Spencer *The Proper Sphere of Government* 1843

Spencer : Herbert Spencer *Social Statistics* 1851

Spencer : Herbert Spencer *The Synthetic Philosophy* 1860-1896

Spencer : Herbert Spencer *The Man versus the State* 1884

Spengler : Oswald Spengler [1880-1936] *The Decline of the West* 1918 volume 1: Form & Actuality [1926—1st English translation] volume 2: Perspectives of World History [1928—1st English translation]

Spengler : Oswald Spengler *The Decline of the West* [abridged version] 1965

Sprague : Irvine H. Sprague *Bailout* [former FDIC chairman tells of mega-bank failures] 1989

Sprague de Camp : See above—Camp.

Spong : John Shelby Spong *Rescuing the Bible from Fundamentalism: a bishop rethinks the Meaning of Scripture* 1991

Spurr : Russell Spurr *Enter the Dragon: china's undeclared war against the U.S. in Korea,* 1950 1951 [in regard to a change in historical perspectives] 1988

St Augustine : See above—Augustine.

Starkey : Marion L. Starkey *The Devil in Massachusetts: a modern enquiry into the Salem witch trials* 1949

Stephenson : Neal Stephenson *Snow Crash* [fiction] 1992 [1993]

Stern : ed, Philip van Doren Stern *The Portable Poe* 1945 [1973] [Besides the general collection of tales includes articles, criticism, letters, poems, an selection of random opinions concerning Poe.]

Stone : Irving Stone *The Passions of the Mind* [biographical fiction of Freud] 1971

Stone : I(sidor) F. Stone *The Hidden History of the Korean War: 1950-1951* [in regard to the public's disregard for journalistic accounts contrary to patriotic fervor] 1952 [1988]

Stowe : Harriet Beecher Stowe [1811-1896] *Uncle Tom's Cabin* [fiction] 1851-52

Sun Tzu : Sun Tzu [circa 4th B.C.E.] *The Art of Warfare* [translation by Roger T. Ames] 1993

Suzuki : D(aisetz) T(eitaro) Suzuki [1870-1966] *Essays in Zen Buddhism* [3 volume series] 1949 / 1953 / 1953

Suzuki & Knudtson : David Suzuki, & Peter Knudtson *Genethics: the clash between the new genetics and human values* 1989

Swift : Jonathan Swift [1667-1745] *Gulliver's Travels* [fiction] 1726

Swisher : Karen L. Swisher, editor *Drug Trafficking* [collection of articles] 1991

Swisher, Karen : See above—O'Neill & Swisher.

Szasz : T(homas) S(tephen) Szasz *Ideology and Insanity* [collection of articles] 1970

Szasz : T(homas) S(tephen) Szasz *The Manufacture of Madness* 1971

Szasz : Thomas S. Szasz *The Myth of mental Illness: foundations of a theory of personal conduct* 1974

• T

Tannahill : Reay Tannahill *Sex in History* 1980

Tanner : Daniel Tanner *Secondary Education: perspectives and prospects* 1972

Taylor : J. J. Taylor *A Retrospect of the Religious Life of England* 1876

Terman : Lewis M. Terman *The Intelligence of School Children* 1919

Thom : James Alexander Thom *Follow the River* [historical fiction] 1981

Thom : James Alexander Thom *From Sea to Shining Sea* [historical fiction] 1984

Thompson : Hunter S. Thompson *Fear and Loathing in Las Vegas* [autobiographical journalism a.k.a. 'gonzo literature'] 1971

Thorne : See above—Misner & Thorne & Wheeler.

Thurow : See above—Heilbroner & Thurow.

Tocqueville : Alexis de Tocqueville [1805-1859] *Democracy in America* [2 volumes] [circa 1840]

Toynbee : Arnold J. Toynbee [1889-1975] *A Study of History* [10 volumes]

3° **Toynbee** : Arnold J. Toynbee [1889-1975] *A Study of History* [abridged to 2 volumes by D. D. Somervell] 1946 [1978]

Truitt : See above—Gould & Truitt.

Turner : See above—Ebenstien & Pritchett & Turner.

Tzu : See above—Sun Tzu.

Tzu : See below—Waltham's *Chuang Tzu…*

• U

UNKNOWN : *Hogen Monogatari* [translation—*Tales of Hogen Civil War* circa 1156]

UNKNOWN : *The Whole Book of Psalmes Faithfully translated into English Metre* 163x

UTOPIAS: Plato's *Republic* , Augustine's *City of GOD*, More's *Utopia*, Bacon's *New Atlantis*, B. F. Skinner's *Walden Two*, Paul Goodman *Utopian Essays and Practical Proposals* [excepting Augustine's '*City of GOD*', & Goodman's '*Essays*' All are works of fiction]

• V

Van Doran : See above—Doran.

Van Horne : James C. Van Horne *Financial Markets: rates and flows* 2nd ed 1978 [1984]

Veblen : Thorstein Veblen [1857-1929] *The Theory of the Leisure Class* 1899 [1912]

Virgil : Virgil Aenid [epic] [circa 36-29 B.C.] [Virgil's lifespan 70-19 B.C.E.]

von Clausewitz : See above—Clausewitz.

von Goethe : See above—Goethe.

von Herder : See above—Herder.

Vonnegut : Kurt Vonnegut, Jr. *Mother Night* [fiction] 1961 [1966]

• W

Walters : See above—Monsen & Walters.

Waltham : Clae Waltham *Chuang Tzu Genius of the Absurd* 1971

Washington : George Washington's 'Diaries'—in regard to entries dated May 12-13, 1765; & August 7, 1765 [Washington's lifespan 1732-1799]

Watts : Alan W. Watts *The Way of Zen* 1957

Watts : Alan W. Watts *The Joyous Cosmology: adventures in the chemistry of consciousness* 1962

Weber : Max Weber [1864-1920] *The Protestant Ethic and the Spirit of Capitalism* [1904-05] 1930

Weber : Max Weber [1864-1920] *The Sociology of Religion* 1922 [1963]

Werthman : See—Cantor & Werthman.

Whalen : Richard J. Whalen *The Founding Father: the story of Joseph P. Kennedy a study in power, wealth, and family ambition* 197x

Wheeler : See above—Misner & Thorne & Wheeler.

Whitcomb & Morris : John C. Whitcomb, JR. & Henry M. Morris *The Genesis Flood: the biblical record and its scientific implications* 1961

Whitehead : See above—Russel & Whitehead.

Whitehouse : H. L. K. Whitehouse *Towards an Understanding of the Mechanism of Heredity* [third edition] 1965 [1973]

Wildavsky : Aaron Wildavsky *The Politics of the budgetary Process* 1964

3° **Williamson** : Marianne Williamson *A Return to Love* 1992 [one of the two main bibles of the New Therapeutic & Sentimental Love Religions. Compare—M. Scott Peck *The Road Less Travelled*]

Williamson : Marianne Williamson *A Woman's Worth* 1993

1° **Wilson** : E. O. Wilson *Sociobiology* 1975

Wilson : L. G. Wilson Sir Charles *Lyell's scientific Journals on the Species Question* 1970

Wilson : Robert Anton Wilson *Nature's GOD* [fiction] 1991

Wilson : Robert Anton Wilson *The Widow's Son* [fiction] 1985 [1989]

Wittgenstein : Ludwig (Josef Johann) Wittgenstein *Tractatus Logico-Philosophicus* 1921

3° **Wolf** : Naomi Wolf *The Beauty Myth* 1991

Wolf: Naomi Wolf *Fire with Fire: the new female power and how it will change the 21st century* 1993

Wolf : Sydney Wolf *Best Pills, Worst Pills* [consumer Reference updated PRN]

Wolfe : Tom Wolfe *The Electric Kool-Aid Acid Test* [autobiographical fiction] 1968 [If you haven't already read this as part of a high school book report, you might try a few pages and see if it fits the well-worn groove of your kool-aid acid testimonial. I include it because it is one of the most stereotypical images of the 'drug-user'. And because Tom, who began writing in the 40s, set about to chronicle the lives and worlds of men in which there is no name for sin. *Bonfire of the Vanities, The Right Stuff,* might ring Pavlov's memory Bell for some of you. And how quickly we forget to, *Look Homeward Angel*]

Wynne : See above—Phillips & Wynne.

• Z

Zaehner : R. C. Zaehner [1913-¿] *Mysticism, Sacred & Profane* 1957

Zahler : Diane Zahler, & Kathy A. Zahler *Test your Cultural Literacy* 1988

Zilbergeld : Bernie Zilbergeld *The Shrinking of America: myths of psychological change* 1983

Zukav : Gary Zukav *The Dancing Wu Li Masters* 1979 [Compare with Fritjof Capra *The Tao of Physics* 197x]

Edited Works

ed, Adrian : E. Adrian (et AL) *Brain Mechanisms and Consciousness* [collection of articles] 1954

ed, Alexander & Selesnick : Franz G. Alexander & Sheldon T. Selesnick *The History of Psychiatry: an evaluation of psychiatric thought and practice from prehistoric times to the present* [an ambitious project which tends to go to sleep in the middle of a thought] 1966

ed, Bernards : Neal Bernards *War on Drugs: opposing viewpoints series* [collection of articles] 1990

ed, Blassingame : John W. Blassingame *Slave Testimony* [Collection of Testimonials] 1977

ed, Brecher : Edward M. Brecher, editor *The Consumers Union Report Licit and Illicit Drugs* [1972]

ed, Capps : Alton C. Capps *The Bible as Literature* 1971

ed, Carey : John Carey *Eyewitness to History* 1987

ed, Coser : Lewis A. Coser *The Pleasures of Sociology* [collection of 36 essays] 1980

eds, Gerstein & Green : Dean R. Gerstein & Lawrence W. Green *Preventing Drug Abuse: what do we know?* 1993

eds, Gould & Truitt : James A. Gould, Willis H. Truitt *Political Ideologies* [collection of essays] 1973 ed, Hamowy : ed, Ronald Hamowy *Dealing with Drugs: consequences of government control* [collection of articles] 1987 [1990] San Francisco : Pacific Research Institute for Public Policy

eds, Kampf & Lauter : Louis Kampf & Paul Lauter *The Politics of Literature: dissenting essays on the teaching of English* [collection of essays—in regard to the control of educational thought & teaching at the university level] 1970 [1972]

eds, Koch & Peden : A. Koch and W. Peden *The Life and Selected Writings of Thomas Jefferson* 1944

eds, Lakatos & Musgrave : Imre Lakatos & Alan Musgrave *Criticism and the Growth of Knowledge* [Collection of personal reflections on Thomas S. Kuhn's short treatise—*The Structure of Scientific Revolutions*] 1970 [1977

eds, Linskens & Jackson : H. F. Linskens, J. F. Jackson *Wine Analysis* 198

ed, Lochner : Louis P. Lochner *The Goebbels Diaries* 1948

ed, Mather : Richard Mather *Bay Psalm Book* 1640

eds, McKeown & McLachlan : Thomas McKeown, Gordon McLachlan *Medical History and Medical Care: a symposium of perspectives* 197

ed, Park : Joe Park *Selected Readings in the Philosophy of Education* [Collection of Essays] 1968

ed, Proger : Samuel Proger *The Medicated Society* 1968 [the ritualization of prescription drug-taking and the creation of its subculture]

ed, Rodgers : Marion Elizabeth Rodgers *The Impossible H. L. Menken* [Collection of news Articles] 1991

ed, Shamos : Morris H. Shamos *Great Experiments in Physics: firsthand accounts from Galileo to Einstein* 1959

ed, Swisher : Karen L. Swisher *Drug Trafficking* [collection of articles] 1991

ed, IN REGARD TO : *The Whole Book of Psalmes Faithfully translated into English Metre* [163x]

REFERENCE, Councils & Commissions

C.P.S.C. a.k.a. Consumer Product Safety Commission—in regard to accident statistics of common everyday household products responsible for more accidents than all drug-related accidents combined

D.O.T. a.k.a. Dept of Transportation—in regard to Title 49 CFR—Part 40 & Part 199.11

G.N.P. a.k.a. Gross National Product—in regard to three misleading treatments

N.A.C a.k.a. Native American Church—in regard to persecution for religious practices

N.I.D.A. a.k.a. National Institute of Drug Abuse—in regard to their statistics

N.S.C. a.k.a. National Safety Council—in regard to accident statistics of common everyday household products responsible for more accidents than all drug-related accidents combined

U.N.E.S.C.O. a.k.a. United Nations Educational, Scientific, & Cultural Organization—in regard to the link between world peace & cultural collapse

O.S.H.A. a.k.a. Occupational Safety & Hazard Association—in regard to forced drug tests

U. S. Bureau of the Census Statistical Abstract of the United States Washington D.C. Government Printing Office. Annual.

U. S. Occupational Hazard Statistics. Washington D.C. Government Printing Office. Annual.

U. S. Office of Scientific Research—in regard to B. F. Skinner, Pigeons, & Bombs.

U. S. Product Safety Commission. Washington D.C. Government Printing Office. Annual.

W.F.B. a.k.a. World Food Bank—in regard to malnourished 'retardation' of 3rd world children

REFERENCE, General

BIBLE: *Today's Parallel Greek-English New Testament* NY: Iverson-Norman Associates 1976 interlined English-Greek text.

CASSELL's NEW GERMAN DICTIONARY German-English Funk & Wagnalls Co 1936

DORLAND's ILLUSTRATED MEDICAL DICTIONARY 25th Edition— in regard to Munchausen's Syndrome. See both Munchausen's & Syndrome.

PHYSICIANS DESK REFERENCE [a.k.a. PDR]—in regard to prescription drug complications; & syndromes [Down's, Ganser, Munchausen's]. Updated annually and with supplements PRN.

MERRIAM WEBSTER's COLLEGIATE DICTIONARY 9th & 10th Editions—all definitions and source words given in main text, may be compared against 10th Edition of Webster's.

ROGET's INTERNATIONAL THESAURUS 1946 [13th printing] Thomas Y. Crowell Publishers

U. S. CONSTITUTION—in regard to the 4th, 5th, & 8th amendments

U. S. CONSTITUTION—in regard to forfeiture

Cushman : CUSHMAN's LEADING CONSTITUTIONAL DECISIONS 13th ed. 1925 [1966]

Findlay : Bruce Allyn Findlay, & Ester Blair Findlay *Your Rugged Constitution* 1950 [1952]—a 270 page reference work with index to the articles, sections, & clauses of the U.S. Constitution. Handy reference for finding a particular cause, etc.

Guinagh : Kevin Guinagh *Dictionary of Foreign Phrases and Abbreviations* 1965 [Nulli secundus! translation—Second to NONE]

Strong : James Strong *THE EXHAUSTIVE CONCORDANCE OF THE BIBLE* 1982 [1986]

eds, *Diagnostic & Statistical Manuel of Mental disorders*—in regard to a catalog of behaviors which seek to codify ethics into suitable knee-jerk responses

eds, *Encyclopedia Britannica* 1974-1994—in regard to complete set for each of these years, mentioning drugs, drug related topics in only superficially positive accounts. And curious lack of mention of historical figures who used or advocated drug-use…

eds, *The anti-Psychiatry Bibliography and Resource Guide* 2nd ed. Vancouver Press: Press Gang Publishers 1979

eds, METZGER & COOGAN, Bruce M. Metzger, & Michael D. Coogan *The Oxford Companion to the Bible* 1993

ed, WILLIAMS, Trevor I. Williams *A BIOGRAPHICAL DICTIONARY of SCIENTISTS* Wiley-inter-science 1969—a good & concise bibliographical reference to the Life & major work of a variety of scientists.

ed, WOLF, Sydney Wolf *Best Pills, Worst Pills* 1994 Updated PRN—in regard to prescription drug complications wrongly associated with natural drugs

ed, ZODHIATES, Spiros Zodhiates *THE HEBREW-GREEK KEY STUDY BIBLE* 1984

Religious Works

All quotes found in main text are from the King James II Version

BIBLE—Corinthians, Deuteronomy, Hosea, Jeremiah, Leviticus, Proverbs, Timothy,—in regard to passages concerning sexuality

BIBLE—Corinthians, Leviticus—in regard to passages concerning homosexuality

BIBLE—in regard to differentiating pride from hubris

BIBLE—in regard to seven deadly sins; ten commandments; Sermon on the Mount; & Sermon on the Plain

BIBLE—Luke—in regard to passage on competent judgment

BIBLE—Sermon on the Mount—in regard to liberation from complete subservience to the group

CATHOLIC ROME's Index of Forbidden Books—in regard to mind censorship

CONCEPTS—Bible, Sutras, Torah—in regard to 'case study' [i.e. casuistry]

CONCEPTS—Pentateuch, Midrash, Mishna, Talmud, Bible, Jurisprudence —in regard to precepts for social conduct and social control

HUMANISTIC SCHOLARSHIP—in regard to the Search for the 'highest levels of humanity'

ISLAM's Closed Gates of Reasoning—an unwritten but acknowledged law of Islamic thought—in regard to mind censorship

JAPAN's Institute for the Investigation of Barbarian Writings—in regard
    to mind censorship

THE QUR'AN [translated by—M. H. Shakir]

Translated Works

• A

Aristotle : Aristotle *The Poetics* [translation by S. H. Butcher, retiled—Aristotle's *Theory of Poetry & Fine Art* 1951]

Aristotle : Aristotle *Nichomachean Ethics* [lifespan of Aristotle 384-323 B.C.E.] NOTE that, in effect, the 'coherence' of Aristotle derives mostly from the juxtaposition of his original lectures by a variety of editors throughout history, including his son Nicomachus. Thus is, it rendered extremely difficult to assign a specific year of publication for any of his works [translation by—Martin Oswald 1962]

Aristotle : Aristotle *Metaphysics* [translated by Hippocrates G. Apostle, includes Commentaries by the Translator 1966 (1979)]

Aristotle : Aristotle *Physics* [translated by Hippocrates G. Apostle, includes commentaries by the Translator 1969 (1980)] [NOTE: these two volumes, The Physics & the Metaphysics I consider to be poor translations as is made evident by the use of terms like—science. A term which wasn't coined until the 14th century. However, the fact that they are poor translations make them excellent flags for the errors inherent in other people's misguided understanding of what Aristotle did or did not suspect about Nature]

Augustine : Saint. Augustine *De Civitate Dei* [circa 413-426 A.D.] [translation—*The City of GOD*]

• B

Bouvoir : Simone De Bouvoir *The Second Sex* [translated from the French by—H. M. Parshley as—*The Second Sex* 1960]

• C

Chardin : Teilhard de Chardin [1881-1955] *Le Phénomene humain* [1938-40] [translated as—*The Phenomenon of Man* 1955]

Clausewitz : Carl von Clausewitz *Vom Kriege* [translation—*On War*]

Comte : Auguste Comte [1798-1857] *Cours de philosophie positive* 6 volumes 1829-1842

• D

Descartes : René Descarte *Regulae* 1701 [translated by Laurence J. LaFleur *Rules for the Direction of the Mind* 1961] [NOTE: this treatise on methodology is incomplete, roughly drafted, and inconsistent. Probably written during winter of 1629, more as a self-reference than as an intended publication]

• E

Ellul : Jacque Ellul *La Technique ou l'enjeu du siecle* 1954 [translation by— John Wilkinson—*The Technological Society* 1964]

Ellul : Jacque Ellul *L'Illusion politique* 1965 [translation by—Konrad Kellen—*The Political Illusion* 1967]

Ellul : Jacque Ellul *Le Systeme technicien* 1977 [translation—*The Technological System* 1980]

Ellul : Jacque Ellul *Propagandes* 1962 [translation by Konrad Kellen & Jean Lerner—*Propaganda* 1973]

Ellul : Jacque Ellul *Violence: reflections from a Christian perspective* [translated by—Cecelia Gaul Kings 1969]

Ellul : Jacques Ellul *Politique de Dieu, Polititques del'homme* 1966 [translated by—Geoffrey W. Bromiley—*The Politics of GOD, the Politics of Man* 1972 (1977)]

• F

Freud : Sigmund Freud *Die Traumdeutung* 1899 [translated by—James Strachey *The Interpretation of Dreams* 1965]

Freud : Sigmund Freud *Der Witz und seine Beziehung zum Unbewussten* 1905 [translated by—James Strachey *Jokes and their Relation to the unconscious* 1960]

Freud : Sigmund Freud *Das Unbehagen in der Kultur* 1930 [translation by—Joan Riviere—*Civilization and its Discontents* 1958]

Froebel : Friedrich Froebel *A Family Book for developing the self Activity of Children* 1845

Froebel : Friedrich Froebel *The Education of Man* 1826

• G

Galilei : Galileo Galilei *Dove ne i congressi di quattro giornate si discorre sopra i due massimi sistemi del mondo tolemaico e copernicano* [translation—*Dialogue concerning the two chief world Systems—Ptloemaic and Copernican*] 1632 [1953]

Galilei : Galileo Galilei *Discorsi e dimostrazioni mathematiche intorno a due nuove scienze attenenti alla meccanica* [translation—*Dialogue concerning Two New Sciences...*] 1638 [1914]

Godement : Godement *Algebra* [translated from the French—*Algebra*] [Houghton Mifflin Publishers] 19xx

Goebbels : (Paul) Joseph Goebbels *Wesen und Gestalt des National Soczialismus* [1935] [literal translation—*Essence and Form in National Socialism*]

Goebbels : (Paul) Joseph Goebbels : Louis P. Lochner, editor *The Goebbels Diaries* 1948

Goethe : Johann (Wolfgang von) Goethe *Die Leiden des Jungen Werthers* 1774 [fiction] [translation by Elizabeth Mayer & Lousie Bogan - *The Sorrows of Young Werther* 1971]

• H

Heidegger : Martin Heidegger [1889-1976] *Kant und das Problem der Metaphysik* 1931 [translated by—James S. Churchill *Kant and the Problem of Metaphysics* 1962]

Herbart : Johann Friedrich Herbart *A Textbook in Psychology* 1894

Herbart : Johann Friedrich Herbart *Outline of Pedagogical Lectures* 1835

Herbart : Johann Friedrich Herbart *Outlines of Education Doctrine* 1901

Herbart : Johann Friedrich Herbart *The Science of Education* 1806

Herder : Johann (Gottfried von) Herder Von Deutshcher *Art und Kunst* [translation—Of German *Art and Artifice*]

Hitler : Adolf Hitler *Mein Kampf* 1925 [translation by—Ralph Manheim 1943]

Jung : C. G. Jung *The undiscovered Self* [translated from the German by R. F. C. Hull 1957]

• K

Kant : Immanuel Kant *Der einzig mögliche beweisgrund zu einer Demonstration des Daseins Gottes* 1762 translated by Gorden Treash as—*The one possible Basis for a Demonstration of the Existence of GOD* 1979 (1994)]

Kant : Immanuel Kant *Kritik der Reinen Vernunft* 1781 [translated by—J. M. D. Meiklejohn *Critique of pure Reason* 1990]

Kant : Immanuel Kant *Religion innerHalb der Grenzen der Blossen Vernunft* 1793 [translated by—Theodore M. Greene, & Hoyt H. Hudson— *Religion within the limits of reason alone* 1934]

• L

Lombroso : Cesare Lombroso *L'uomo delinquente* 1876 [translation *The Criminal Man*]

Lucretius : Titus Lucretius Carus [circa 96-55 B.C.] *De Rerum Natura* [translation by Charles E. Bennett *On the Nature of Things* 1946]

• M

Maimonides : Moses Maimonides [1135-1204] Arabic title—*Dalalat al-Hairin* [Hebrew title—*Moreh Nebuchim*] 1135-1168 [translation by M. Friedländer—*The Guide for the Perplexed* 1904]

Marivaux : Pierre (Carlet de Champlain de) Marivaux *La Vie de Marianne* 1731-41 [fiction] [translation—*The Life of Marianne*]

Marx & Engels : Karl Marx & Friedrich Engels *Manifest der Kommunistischen Partei* 1848 [translated by Samuel Moore—*The Communist Manifesto* 1964]

Molina : Tirso de Molina *El Burlador de Sevilla* [fiction] [translated as— *The Love Rogue*] 1630

Monmouth : Geoffry of Monmouth [died 1155] *Historia Regum Britannicae* [translation—*History of the Kings of Britain*]

Montaigne : Michel de Montaigne *Essais* 1580 [translated by—J. M. Cohen—*Essays* 1981]

More : Thomas More *Concerning the best State of a commonwealth and the new Island of Utopia* 1518 [translated from the Latin by—Robert M. Adams as—*Utopia: a new translation, backgrounds, criticism* 1975] [See also—UTOPIAS]

• N

Nietzsche : Friedrich Nietzsche [1844-1900] *Also sprach Zarathustra* 1883-85 [translated by R. J. Hollingdale—*Thus spake Zarathustra* Penguin 1961]

Nietzsche : Friedrich Nietzsche [1844-1900] *Der Wille zur Macht* 1901/1910-11 [translated by Walter Kaufmann as—*The Will to Power in Basic Writings of Nietzsche* 1968]

• P

Pacioli : Lucas Pacioli *Summa de Arithmetica, Geometria, Proportioni and Proportionalita* 1494

Plato : Plato *Politeia* [circa 384-370 B. C.] [translation—*The Republic*]

Plato : Plato *Apologia, Crito, & Euthyphro* circa 399 B.C.E. [translated & rearranged by—Hugh Tredennick—retitled *The last Days of Socrates* 1954]

Popper : Karl R(aimund) Popper *Logik der Forschung* 1934 [translated by—Julius Freed, Lan Freed, & Karl Popper—*The Logic of Scientific Discovery* 1959]

Prévost : Eugene-Marcel Prévost *Les Demi-Vierges* 1894 [fiction] [*The Half Virgins*]

• S

Sade : Marquis de Sade [Comte Donatien-Alphonse-François] *La Histoire Juliette* [circa] 1797 [translated by—Austryn Wainhouse published as—*Juliette* 6 volumes in one 1968]

Samhaber : Ernst Samhaber *Merchants Make History* [translated from German by—E. Osers] 1960 [1964] [first comprehensive history of trade & commerce illustrating that trade precedes the flag of nations in contact between societies & civilizations]

Sartre : Jean-Paul Sartre *L'être et le néant* 1943 [translated by—Hazel E. Barnes *Being and Nothingness: a phenomenological essay on ontology* 1956]

Spengler : Oswald Spengler *Der Untergang des abendlandes* / *The Decline of the West* 1918 [volume 1—*Gestalt & Wirklichkeit* / *Form & Actuality* 1926] [volume 2—*WeltHistorische Perspektiven* / *Perspectives of World History* 1928]

Spengler : Oswald Spengler *Der Untergang des Abendlandes, Gekürzte Ausgabe* 1959 [translated by ??? published by Modern Library:

Random House as—*The Decline of the West* , abridged version 1961 (1965)]

Sophocles : Sophocles *Oedipus Rex* [fiction] [translation- *Oedipus the King*]

Sun Tzu: Sun Tzu *The Art of Warfare* [Translation by Roger T. Ames] 1993

• U

UNKNOWN : *Hogen Monogatari* [translation—*Tales of Hogen Civil War* circa 1156]

• V

IN REGARD TO : *The Whole Book of Psalmes Faithfully translated into English Metre* 163x

IN REGARD TO : *The Qur'an* [translated by—M. H. Shakir] 1991

Virgil : Virgil *Aenid* [epic] [circa 36-29 B.C.]

• W

Weber : Max Weber *Die Protestantische Ethik und der Geist des Kapitalismus* [1904-05] [translation—*The Protestant Ethic and the Spirit of Capitalism*] 1930

Weber : Max Weber *Religions Soziologie,* from *Wirtschaft und Gesellschaft* 1922 [translated by—Ephraim Fischoff—*The Sociology of Religion* 1963]

Index

0-595-24841-1

www.ingramcontent.com/pod-product-compliance
Lightning Source LLC
Chambersburg PA
CBHW061346280526
45784CB00001B/159